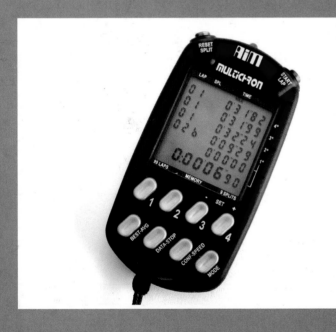

EVERYTHING YOU NEED TO KNOW

KARTING

JEFF GRIST and MEMO GIDLEY

MOTORBOOKS

First published in 2006 by Motorbooks, an imprint of MBI Publishing Company, Galtier Plaza, Suite 200, 380 Jackson Street, St. Paul, MN 55101-3885 USA

ISBN-13: 978-0-7603-2345-8
ISBN-10: 0-7603-2345-3

Editor: Jennifer Johnson
Designer: Brenda C. Canales

Printed in China

On the cover: Memo Gidley paces a Trackmagic Dragon powered by a Yamaha YF200R1 at Moran Raceway in Beaumont, California. Memo is wearing a karting suit from design 500 Racewear and Bell Fueling helmet painted by Corby Concepts. *Sean Burr,* GO Racing Magazine

On the frontispiece: Speedway kart racing on a dirt tracks draw large fields of racers. *Rowdy Jordan*

On the title pages: *(left to right)* Mychron Stopwatch from Aimsports.

An X5 disk clutch from Horstman Clutches.

World Formula engine by Briggs & Stratton.

Memo Gidley measures a Bridgestone kart racing slick tire.

On the back cover: *(Top right)* Robert Wickens in action at the Barrie Grand Prix held in Barrie, Ontario, Canada. *Teresa Matkovich*

(Bottom right) Arrive and Drive racing action at Adams Kart Track in Riverside, California. *Sean Buur*

(Left) Junior cage kart action in the WKA Heartland Speedway Series. *Rowdy Jordan*

About the authors:
Memo Gidley is professional race car driver currently competing in the ROLEX Daytona Prototype Sports Car series with the Finley Motorsports No. 19 Air Force Reserve/Make-A-Wish racing team. Memo has over 12 years of professional car racing experience at the highest levels, including CHAMP Car, Prototype Sports Cars, IRL, and Trans Am. Memo began his motorsports career in Northern California racing karts in the KT100 pipe class for Trackmagic Racing Karts of San Francisco, California. Before moving to cars, Memo won two Super National 125cc Gearbox championships and numerous regional championships in various classes.

Memo currently lives in Novato, California, and commutes to Charlotte, North Carolina, where the Finley Motorsports team is based. Memo is the co-founder of Secrets of Speed Publications Inc. and the co-author of three previous books on karting and kart racing.

Jeff Grist is a karting and motorsports enthusiast having competed in both motocross and karting. He is the President of PromoSpyder Inc., an interactive marketing agency focusing on motorsports. Jeff has over 20 years of professional marketing experience with companies like TRW Automotive, Stanley Tools, and Canadian Duty Free, where he developed numerous motorsports support programs.

Jeff currently lives in Grimsby, Ontario, Canada, with his wife Helen and son Garett. He is the co-founder of Secrets of Speed Publications Inc. and the co-author of three previous books on karting and kart racing.

CONTENTS

Acknowledgments

Co-author Jeff Grist with his wife Helen.

Since Memo and I first decided to start writing books for karting, we have had a great deal of support from the entire karting industry. Many people have helped us put this book and our three Secrets of Speed books together. Without the support, encouragement, and insight from all of these individuals, we could not have achieved the incredible success our book series currently enjoys

We would like to extend a special thank you to Donnie Graves for helping us along the way and encouraging us to start this journey. Also a BIG thanks to Fausto Vitello of Trackmagic Racing Karts for his fantastic support, Art Verlengiere of RLV Exhuasts for is tremendous encouragement, and Dan Wilson of Briggs and Stratton Motorsports for his incredible generosity.

We would also like to recognize the many other companies that have provided products and information to our program over the years. AimSports, Alpinestars Racewear, Andersen Pit Karts, Bell Racing Helmets, Bridgestone Tires, Burris Racing, Corby Concepts, Cytomax Energy Drinks, DecalWorks, Design 500 Racewear, Douglas Wheels, Horstman Clutches, KG Bodywork, Longacre Scales, Odenthal Manufacturing, PACE American Trailers, Prospeed Kartsports, ROTAX Racing Engines, Sniper Alignment Systems, Swedetech Racing Engines, Tillett Racing Seats, TM Racing Engines, Torco Lubricants, and Yamaha Kart Racing.

Memo and I have been fortunate enough to work with some of the best photographers in the business. These incredible shooters include Sean Burr of *GO Racing Magazine*, Jeff Deskins of Shift Sport Imagery, Peter Frey of Finlay Motorsports, Bernd Fuchs of Bernd Fuchs Photography, Rowdy Jordan of P&R Photos, Theresa Matkovich of Photo Arts International, and Todd McCall of On Track Promotions. Thanks for your great photographs and for helping put this book together. We would like to recognize Craig Ketchen of Pillar Design for his awesome illustrations and his hard work helping us get our books done.

Every project has a special person who contributes a sense of friendship and commitment. For Memo and I that person is Earl Ma. Earl has documented Memo's rise in professional car racing and has helped organize Memo's karting clinic in Hawaii. Earl's battle with illness and his continuing commitment to our program make him a very special person to us. Get well soon.

Finally a BIG thank you to our families for all of their support and encouragement. Sorry for the late nights and long hours. You guys are the best.

—Jeff Grist

Introduction

This book is all about learning the basics of karting and how to get started. Karting is an exciting motor sport that the entire family can enjoy. What makes karting special is that there are so many variations; no matter where you live or what your personal taste may be, there is likely to a type of karting for you.

What also makes karting standout from other motorsports is that you can enjoy it as a stepping-stone into professional racing or for a lifetime as a hobby. For me, karting was a way to reach my goal of becoming a professional race car driver, while for my co-author Jeff Grist, karting is a family activity as they spend their weekends watching their son Garett race.

What follows is a book that will be your guide into the world of karting. On the outside looking in, karting may seem like a complicated sport. However, in this book we will make the process of getting into karting easy and simple to understand. We will explain the many classes of karting and the different racing formats to help find a class that's interesting and exciting to you. From buying your first kart, to driving to your first day at the track, all the way to fine tuning your kart for peak performance, this book can be used to help you plan out your steps into the sport at the pace that's right for you.

Not only will this book will give you a solid basic understanding of all those aspects of karting, it will also save you time and money by quickly pointing you in the right direction when first venturing into the karting world. If there is one area of karting

Co-author Memo Gidley

that's lacking, it's having good, current information that's available for the first time driver that is written by people who know and have the experience.

In this book you will not only find information from my experiences from when I first began in Kart racing, but also things that I have continued to learn throughout my racing career. There is also information from Jeff Grist, an avid recreational karter and one of the top karting how-to book authors who has made kart racing part of his and his family's way of life for the past 10 years. With all the experience and information in this book, you have a comprehensive and easy-to-understand karting book that will be in a class of its own.

—Memo Gidley

Chapter 1

LET'S GO KARTING

Top North American drivers take to the track in Austin, Texas, for the STARS of Karting series finale. *Sean Buur*

There's a form of karting and a level of competition for every age group.

WHAT IS KARTING ALL ABOUT?

Karting is a fun, fast-paced motorsport that's enjoyable for the entire family. Like many outdoor adventure activities, it's a great way to spend time with friends and family in a safe, fun environment. Karting is a sport you can do for life and pass on to generations to come. It combines camping with competition to make a true learning experience.

As you will see, we are firm believers in being prepared *before* you get to the racetrack. Karting is more than just driving; it's about working on your kart and setting goals. Karting tests all your skills, both physical and mental. For some, karting is a fun activity. For others, it's a step toward bigger things in the world of motorsports.

Levels of Karting

There's a form of karting and a level of competition for every age group. Many racers love the thrill and fun of local club racing. Being part of a race club is a great way to meet new friends and participate at an affordable level. From the local club scene you can participate at the regional level, which brings together the best competition from around your state or province. With regional racing comes stiffer competition and higher costs associated with traveling longer distances. Also, there is the added pressure of learning new tracks and kart setups.

For an elite few, there is national-level competition such as the STARS of Karting. These series cover the entire country and brings together the best the sport has to offer, including drivers from other countries. All the major manufacturers participate with their factory-supported teams and drivers. These events are run over several days with many racers racing in different classes.

Road to Racing Cars

For some drivers, karting is the starting point to a motorsports career. Many well-known car-racing champions from many different series have come from karting. These include drivers not only here in North America but also from many parts of globe. Names like Jeff Gordon, Paul Tracy, Michael Schumacher, Tony Stewart, and this book's coauthor, Memo Gidley, all started their careers in karting. Karting allows young drivers to develop their driving skills and race craft at an early age. Learning good race craft and

Above: **Karting can be enjoyed by both boys and girls, young and old alike. The friendships that come with karting will last a lifetime.** *Sean Buur*

Left: **Memo Gidley has turned successful karting into a career, including two National Championships, into a professional car racing career. Here he is at the ROLEX 24 Hours of Daytona, racing in the prototype category.** *Earl Ma*

ACCESSIBILITY

Karting is one of the few motorsports that offers accessibility to wheelchair-bound athletes. One of the original goals of the Full Circle Foundation was to produce a go kart that would fit into the mainstream world of karting so that those who are wheelchair bound could race or just ride for fun on an equal basis. The newest design incorporates specially designed hand-operated controls (HOC) for the brake and throttle, along with a seat designed around the driver's "seat." The material used makes the seat much more comfortable for physically challenged drivers.

Make no mistake: these HOC karts are serious machines! Child versions can reach speeds of 40 miles per hour, and adult versions go as fast as 70 to over 100 miles per hour. To those involved in Full Circle Foundation karting, there is nothing more rewarding than seeing the smile on the face of someone who is experiencing the heart-pumping action of controlling this machine and forgetting their physical disability.

Taking to the track in a hand-operated-controls (HOC) kart is a great way for disabled athletes to enjoy the fun and thrills of motorsports. *Todd McCall*

Drivers need to be in good physical condition to drive and cope with up to 2.5 g forces and extreme heat.

understanding motorsports safety at an early age are key to developing a strong professional career. The skills learned on and off the karting track can be transferred to car racing. It is this long history of driver progression that fuels the intense interest in karting. Who knows? You may be racing with the next world champion.

Physical Demands

Karting can be enjoyed from age 8 to 80, but it is an active sport that can be very physically demanding. Quick reflexes and good vision are critical to success in karting. Drivers need to be in good physical condition to drive and cope with up to 2.5 g forces and extreme heat. Before you begin karting be sure to check with your doctor. Important areas of the body to condition for strength include shoulders, arms, and back. Most people new to karting are surprised by just how physical it really is to drive one of these machines.

HISTORY OF KARTING

The man most often credited with building the first modern-style kart is Art Ingles. A race car builder, Art was an American airman stationed in Europe during World War II. As a pastime, he and other American pilots built small vehicles from metal tubes to drive during their free time. Upon returning home to the United States, Art built a kart using semipneumatic tires, a West Bend two-stroke engine, a steering system, and a chain-and-sprocket drive. He first demonstrated his creation in 1956 in a supermarket parking lot in Los Angeles.

By 1957, Art and others, like Duffy Livingstone, began holding impromptu races in the parking lot of the Rose Bowl in Pasadena, California. Soon after, drivers began to develop innovative designs like the DRONE, so named because the engine was originally used in a U.S. Army radio-controlled drone airplane. The karts and speeds quickly outgrew parking lots and before long, karting tracks began to appear throughout Southern California and the sport of karting was born. The name "Go Kart" can be traced back to a company called GP Mufflers, which, after seeing Art Ingles' original creation, created its own versions of karts, which they continued to improve.

In 1958, the Go Kart Club of America was incorporated in California, followed by the creation of the American Kart Manufacturer's Association in 1959. It was these two groups that drove the industry forward and helped to build strong grassroots popularity. Many large races were staged throughout the late 1950s and early 1960s, helping to spread the word about karting across the United States.

During the 1960s, 1970s, and 1980s, karting enjoyed many ups, as well as suffered from many downs. Throughout this period, brave pioneers continued to develop new kart designs as the sport progressed, and the main center of karting began to shift away from the United States to Europe. Many of today's major chassis and engine builders are located in Europe, with the strongest concentration in Italy.

From its very inception, karting has been part of the CIK/FIA world governing body of motorsport. Karting has benefited greatly as a recognized part of the motorsports community, allowing a clear path for racers to follow to the top levels of motorsports. The CIK/FIA has also helped karting safety through the decades. Many current car racing standards and procedures for track and vehicle safety have been adapted to karting.

BASIC LAYOUT OF A KART

Today's karts have evolved from the early days of Art Ingles and his many peers and now very much resemble automobiles in format and operation. What makes karting so fun and dynamic is having this direct connection to the amazing race cars we see on TV or at the track. As you learn more about karting, you will deal with many of the same set-up and driving issues you hear professional race car drivers talk about.

The simplicity of a kart's design is based on metal tubing that is bent and welded together to form the frame or chassis. The basic design of any kart chassis uses a solid axle, or live axle as it is sometimes called, which locks the rear wheels together by way of a single axle. By contrast, a race car uses a differential in the rear end. Differential allows the inside wheel to rotate less than the outside wheel as they travel through a different radius which helps the car turn easier through a corner. A kart relies on weight jacking and

The basic design of any kart chassis uses a solid axle.

Karting has been part of the CIK/FIA world governing body of motorsport.

50TH ANNIVERSARY

2006 marks the official 50th anniversary of karting. The Karting Industry Council, the oldest and largest trade association for the sport in North America, held a contest to design a new logo to mark the special occasion. The winning logo was designed by artist Justin Jacobs of Lake City, Kansas, and was selected from 57 logos submitted by various artists from around the world. Designers from the United States, Canada, and other countries including Great Britain, Bangladesh, and Serbia submitted entries. Judges for the contest included members of the print and electronic karting media from North America and Europe.

The logo will be used by Karting Industry Council to commemorate the 50th anniversary of the sport in print, on apparel, and on other mediums, with all proceeds going to the non-profit trade association. As an independent organization, the Karting Industry Council acts as a liaison between the karting industry and karting organizations, clubs, and track owners.

This overhead shot shows the basic layout of a sprint kart. The engine is mounted on the right side and the driver seat is slightly to the left. All kart formats have the gas pedal mounted on the right and the brake pedal on the left. The steering wheel runs up from the front. *Sean Buur*

A well-installed and properly fitted seat means a faster kart.

separately allows the driver to react more quickly. The pedals are mounted at the very front of the chassis and use a simple round tubing design. The pedal position can be adjusted to suit the driver's size.

Engine

Kart engines are mounted on the driver's right side near the back end of the kart. This allows the engine to be close to the rear axle to drive the kart forward. Kart-racing engines can be both two-stoke and four-stoke and can range from 4 to 50-plus horsepower. The most common two-stroke engines are 100-cc air-cooled engines that will produce about 12 horsepower. The most common four-stroke engines are made by Briggs & Stratton, which, with some modifications, can produce up to 10 horsepower.

chassis flex to allow the inside rear wheel to lift off the ground and help the kart turn through corners.

Pedals

Like the average automobile, a kart has a gas pedal and a brake pedal. Most karts are clutch driven so when you press on the gas pedal, the clutch engages and off you go. For some karts, a clutch lever mounted to the steering wheel is used to engage the engine. The big difference between a car and a kart is braking with your left foot. Many first-time karters struggle with this, but with practice it becomes familiar. Controlling the brake and gas

Seat

The seat is one of the most critical components of a kart because it connects the largest mass, you, the driver, to the kart. Too often the seat is improperly positioned or poorly installed, directly affecting the handling performance of the chassis. A well-installed and properly fitted seat means a faster kart.

Like the geometry and flex built into the chassis, kart manufacturers spend a lot of time testing for proper seat positioning. Most manufacturers will

Gary Carlton uses a hand-held electric start to fire a Yamaha YF200R1 for Memo Gidley. Karts use a variety of starting systems, including onboard electric starts and side-cover–mounted pull cord starters. *Sean Buur*

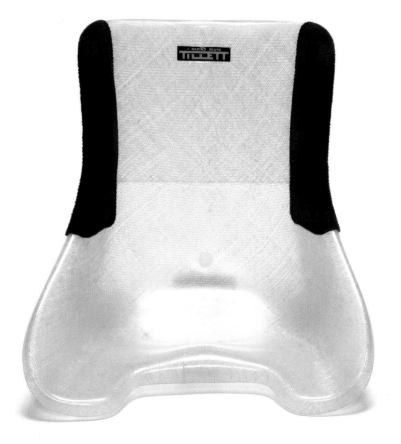

Most kart seats are made from fiberglass or plastic and should be positioned to ensure the driver is comfortable. *Sean Buur*

Speedway karts use large bodywork to cover the wheels, allowing for close, tight racing on small oval tracks. Drivers sit low in the kart to keep the center of gravity low. *Rowdy Jordan*

It's important to keep your brakes clean and free from dirt and grease.

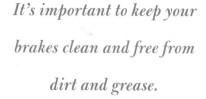

have recommended settings for optimum performance. These are available from your dealer or from the manufacturer's website. You should always consult your chassis manufacturer or your seat manufacturer for exact mounting specifications. We will go into more detail on seat setup in Chapter 5.

Brakes

Most karts make use of a single rear brake that is mounted on the rear axle. The pedal pulls on an arm that moves a hydraulic pump system. Faster karts such as shifter karts and super karts also have front brake systems. The brake system on a kart is lightweight and uses pad-and-rotor setups similar to a car's. It's important to keep your brakes clean and free from dirt and grease, and keep an eye on your brake pads to make sure they're not worn out.

Tires

Like a race car, the tires on a kart are tubeless, that is, the air is held inside the tire with a tight seal between the tire bead and the wheel rim. Karts use slicks for dry weather and grooved tires for wet weather. When you look at the size of a kart tire in relation to the overall weight of the kart, you get a good understanding of why karts perform so well. The combination of being lightweight and having a lot of rubber makes for high levels of grip. Racing kart tires are low and wide, compared with other racing tires. This allows a kart to have a short sidewall, which creates a tire that reacts quickly to driver input.

Wheels

Rims are also a key component of the entire wheel assembly. They can be made from stamped aluminum, machined from billet stock, or cast from magnesium. The high amount of grip generated by karts puts a tremendous strain on the rims. This high grip builds up heat, which plays a big role in tire performance. Each type of rim material will handle heat buildup differently. Some rims are also designed to be stiffer than others, and this can also have an effect on the handling of the kart. A stiffer or softer rim will have a similar effect to a stiffer or softer frame. The lower the grip or smoother the track,

the stiffer a rim you might want; the higher the grip or the bumpier track, the softer the rim you might choose. All karts use a three-bolt pattern for mounting rear tires.

European-made components, however, use a different bolt-pattern standard from those made in the United States. Most karts use a front rim with the bearing built in; the wheel simply

All karts use a disc brake system. While most modern systems are hydraulic, like the one pictured here, still some kid karts use a mechanical style. *Sean Buur*

Speedway karts will use "offset," meaning the left wheel is in closer to the frame than the right wheel. This helps the kart turn easier through corners. *Rowdy Jordan*

Kart rims come in various sizes and finishes. Some front wheels have a spindle bearing, while others use a three-bolt pattern with a spindle hub. *Sean Buur*

A dealer that can provide track support is very important.

slides onto the front spindle. In some cases, a spindle hub is used, so the front rim will use a three-bolt pattern. Shifter Karts using front brakes use a special spindle hub with the brake rotor attached. A special wheel hub is used to adjust the front end. These hubs also use a three bolt pattern.

GETTING STARTED IN KARTING

The sport of karting has experienced dramatic growth over the past two decades, marked not only by increased participation, but also by an increase in the number of karting facilities. While only a small percentage of karters become professional racers, many drivers from all levels of motorsports race karts to keep their skills honed, or simply because they love it. Karting is very much a family sport; everyone can get involved in the day's activities. The first step to starting any new hobby or sport is gaining the proper knowledge. It's important to gather as much

information as possible to help understand the world of karting. The best sources of information are your local kart track, magazines, and the Internet.

The karting industry has a number of good consumer magazines available by subscription and on the newsstand. A subscription to one or more of these magazines is a good way to learn about karting. Many of these monthly magazines list clubs, provide technical articles, highlight drivers and karts, and provide classified ads. Magazines that provide coverage of karting include *Go Racing*, *KartSport*, *National Kart News*, and *Superkart Illustrated*.

By far the best way to learn about karting is to attend races at your local track. You will find plenty of racers anxious to tell you about their karts and their racing experiences. It's important to learn what class of karts race in your area, and which are supported by local dealerships. It's best to consider a popular class so that no matter how fast

or slow you may be, there will always be someone to race with. Racing is all about mixing it up with others and small grids rarely make for fun racing. The class or level you race with should be your guide to the kind of equipment you will need. Be careful when choosing your equipment. While most karts look somewhat similar to one another, each is intended for a specific class, and costs and speeds vary widely.

BUYING A KART

Before you jump into purchasing your kart, be sure to set a reasonable budget. Check out the classified ads in the back of karting magazines and online to get a good sense of how much the kart/engine combination you are

looking for would cost. You can purchase your kart new or used. Each has pros and cons.

Purchasing new from a dealer will get you what is commonly referred to as a roller. This is a complete kart with seat, steering wheel, body, and rims. The engine and tires are extra, as they will need to be specific to the class you intend to race. Some dealers sell complete karts or ready-to-race packages that include an engine and tires—all you need to do is add gas and oil and go. It is best to find a dealer that's been in business for a long time and has a strong clientele. Also, a dealer that can provide trackside support is very important. And don't forget to let the dealer know where you intend to race so

This typical four-stroke sprint kart setup uses Yamaha YF200R1 engine on a Trackmagic Dragon chassis. Before buying a new or used kart, put it on a stand so you can see the all the components and get a good look at the frame. *Sean Buur*

they can put together the right package. The plus side to buying from a dealer is the kart is new and set up for you. You know the frame is straight and there are no bent or worn parts. The down side is that you don't get any spares like tie rods, spindles, or axles. These are components that you will need at some point and will add to your cost.

Purchasing used from a local racer can be a great way to go. The kart will usually be complete and come with many spares and extras. It's great to find a driver who is moving up to a new class or a different type of racing. They usually sell everything that goes with their kart. You want to look for a clean, well-maintained kart. Be sure to ask if the kart has been crashed and has

suffered any major damage. Also ask if the frame has ever been straightened. Be sure to flip the kart up and look at the underside. This will tell you a lot about how hard the kart has been raced and whether there has been major wear and tear from driving off the track.

Whether buying a new or a used kart, be sure that it will not only meet your needs today, but down the road as well. If you're in the last year of a class and must move up next year, be sure that your frame or engine can still be used. Ideally you don't want to have to change karts after one season. Also check with the racing organization to see if any rule changes are planned for the coming season. This is usually not an issue at the club level but can be a

Karting has greatly expanded its reach by introducing unique events like the Rock Island Grand Prix, held on the downtown streets of Rock Island, Illinois. This event draws spectators from all over the Midwest. *Sean Buur*

RACING ORGANIZATIONS

Throughout North America and the world there are hundreds of racing organizations running many different karting classes. We have selected a few of the larger, longer-standing organizations with large membership bases to focus on. These organizations have a good track record of operating fun, safe races at proper karting venues. All of these are based in the United States, but many have international associations and represent a good cross section of karting.

The World Karting Association (WKA) is a membership-owned, non-profit corporation formed in 1971 to regulate and promote the sport of competitive kart racing. It establishes the rules and sets standards by which to sanction tracks and conduct annual championships for various types of karting. WKA has grown to over 10,000 active members and 120 sanctioned tracks nationwide, making it the largest sanctioning body for kart racing in the United States and one of the largest in the world. For more information go to www.worldkarting.com.

The International Kart Federation (IKF) takes pride in its long record of achievement as a governing body for the sport of kart racing. In recognition of the need for controls over the sport, the IKF has published rules for competition since November 21, 1957. Throughout this time, the objectives of the Federation have been the same: to foster strong and fair competition; to provide reasonable rules for the various types of competition; to administer the competition program with impartiality; and to reduce the hazards associated with this sport. For more information go to www.ikfkarting.com.

The Snap-on STARS of Karting series' goal is to promote and bring awareness to karting. The series, founded three years ago by Bryan Herta and the late Hollis Brown, was developed to provide a starting point for a career in open wheel racing. The STARS of Karting is poised to establish the proper structure and competition in American karting to allow new generations of American racing stars to flourish.

The Snap-on Stars of Karting follows the CIK format of event criteria; their events are run under strict guidelines similar to the rest of the world and allow drivers to compete with karters from around the world.

Stars of Karting will offer six classes in 2006, including ICA or Intercontinental A, JICA or Junior Intercontinental, Cadet, and TAG class. For more information, visit www.starsofkarting.com.

The ROTAX MAX Challenge is a kart racing series dedicated to the Rotax engine. The engine used is the FR125 MAX (FR125 Junior for the Junior MAX Challenge) with strictly no modifications allowed. Established in 1997, the ROTAX Kart Center now organizes national competition in over 32 countries, including the United States, Canada, and parts of Europe, among others.

The ROTAX MAX Challenge endeavors to provide, at club level, performance approaching that of conventional 125cc racing karts combined with low running costs and low noise levels. While there is a ROTAX class for every age, the typical ROTAX driver is in their mid-30s and has the need for speed but doesn't want to invest a lot of time or money. These drivers simply want to go racing without the hassles of maintaining fragile race engines. For further information visit www.rmaxchallenge.com.

Superkarts! USA (SKUSA) was formed in 1993 to create an organization specifically for the class of racing karts known as shifter karts" Shifter karts are a development of the typical racing karts that trace their roots back to the early 1950s. The replacement of the usual 100cc kart motor with a 125cc engine/gearbox assembly transforms a Go Kart into a shifter kart. Although primarily focused on shifters, SKUSA now has a complete racing program that includes the TAG USA class. SKUSA runs the TAG class at a number of regional events and a few select national events like the Supernationals held in Las Vegas, Nevada. For more information, go to www.skusaonline.com.

---

major factor at the regional and national levels.

Whether you purchased your kart new from a dealer or used from a local driver, it's now your kart. It is your responsibility to make sure the kart is safe to drive. Don't rely on someone else. You need to check the mounting of all components to make sure everything is tight and secure. It is very important that you become familiar with how your kart is put together. This will give you an idea of how to fix your kart when a repair is needed. Your first on-track outing should be pure orientation. You need to make sure that your kart is properly broken in

and use this time to see if anything in the installation process was overlooked. You do not want to rush this process to get a quick lap time. Also, use this first run as a chance to get familiar with how your new kart feels and responds on the track.

After you have purchased a new kart, your chassis manufacturer can be a good source for information. Go to their website and get all the information you can on your make and model. Your local kart dealer should be able to supply other key information, like a baseline chassis and seat-mounting setup. Don't be afraid to ask questions. Also, you need to build a dialogue with

It is your responsibility to make sure the kart is safe to drive.

KARTING MAGAZINES AND WEB SITES

The karting industry has a number of good consumer magazines available by subscription and on the newsstand. A subscription to one or more of these magazines is a good way to learn about karting. Many of these monthly magazines list clubs, provide technical articles, highlight drivers and karts, and provide classified ads. The following magazines provide coverage of four-cycle sprint karting.

Go Racing

Go Racing magazine was originally started in Southern California to give the local racers a monthly outlet for upcoming events, and series. Since then, it has grown, along with the sport. *Go Racing* differs from other magazines by its free distribution to kart clubs, kart tracks, and kart shops throughout the United States. Clubs that have requested to be on the distribution list are sent magazines, to be made available on race day for their members. Home delivery subscriptions are also available for $26 in the United States if you would rather the magazine be sent to your house. Although the primary focus is on sprint racing, *Go Racing* covers the entire sport of karting. Sprint, road racing, speedway, and both two- and four-cycle racing can be found in *Go Racing* throughout the year.

For subscription information call (909) 930-5045 or visit www.goracingmagazine.com.

KartSport

Widely recognized as the voice of the karter in the paddock, *KartSport* is entertaining, controversial, addictive, and thought-provoking, as well as the only kart magazine to travel the world and bring readers the full expanse of this global sport. From Las Vegas to Wisconsin to Ontario, from Daytona to Vancouver to Illinois, from Italy to South Africa to Mexico, *KartSport* is always on hand to showcase karting as the newest member of the action sports industry. The heart of each monthly issue of *KartSport* is a blend of interviews with the sport's most intriguing personalities, event coverage, and superb photography.

For subscription information call toll-free (888) 520-9099 Monday through Friday, 8 a.m. to 4:30 p.m. (PST), or visit www.kartsportmag.com.

National Kart News

Since 1986, *National Kart News* has been the magazine of choice for both professional and recreational kart racers. From the ultra-extreme shifter karts, to the exciting world of four-cycle oval racing, *NKN* covers it all. Whether your interest is in learning more about the technical aspect of the sport, or wanting to learn what happened at a particular race in Europe, you'll find all that and more in each issue of *National Kart News*.

For subscription information call Toll Free 1 (800) 277-0033 or visit www.nkn.com.

Superkart Illustrated

Now in its seventh year of publication, *Super Kart Illustrated* is described as the magazine produced "for kart racers by kart racers." Originally titled *Shifter Kart Illustrated*, this magazine has expanded from its original all-shifter-kart format. *SKI* is unparalleled in its coverage of the sport's action, including shifters, 100cc, TaG, four-cycle, and road racing. Each issue gives readers what they are looking for: insider news, race reports, profiles and interviews, hard-hitting stories, nationwide results, and great technical articles.

For subscription information call (905) 271-3236 or visit www.superkartmag.com.

Another potentially good source for information is the Internet—potentially is said because you do need to be careful. With traditional magazines as listed above, there is an editor to verify that the information is correct and accurate. On the Internet that is not always the case, especially in the area of forums and blogs. Always be careful with the information you gather from the Internet. Take information forums as advice and use with caution. Here is a list of six very good and reputable sites that feature some content on four-cycle racing.

4cycle.com

Also known as Bob's four-cycle, the main focus of this site is speedway or oval kart racing, but it does contain lots of great insight and information on four-cycle engines, especially the Briggs Raptor. A lot of good technical information on engine tuning can be found throughout the site.

briggsracing.com

This site is operated by Briggs & Stratton Racing and contains information on all Briggs racing engines. Especially good are the technical updates and technical specifications on each engine.

burrisracing.com

This site is operated by Burris Racing and includes a section on the F200 program. In this section is an outline of the rules and regulations for the F200 program for Honda, Briggs, Yamaha, and Tecumseh.

ekartingnews.com

Ekartingnews.com is easily the largest and most visited of the karting web sites. It lists many advertisers and has a great listing of race schedules. EKN is the world's most popular karting web site, and is the only site with a dedicated full-time editorial staff. Packed with daily news and information, EKN has become the outright source for on-time news delivery. Trackside segments bring event coverage to another level with results, reports, and photos. EKN provides everything an online karter could want.

worldkarting.com

Operated by the World Karting Association, or WKA, this site helps you gain an understanding of some of the many four-cycle sprint classes available. The WKA is the largest sanctioning body in the sport of karting in North America and has a long history in four-cycle karting for both speedway and sprint.

your engine builder. He will be vital in helping you avoid costly mistakes.

Before you strap on your gear, let's go through a quick general check and baseline setup. Start by putting your kart up on a stand. Don't try to work on the ground as it is easy to miss something. You need to get your tools organized and be ready to go. Be prepared and you won't get sidelined with unnecessary problems or delays.

EQUIPMENT

You'll need some basic equipment to keep your kart in top shape. These items are critical to ensure that your kart is safe and fun to drive.

Kart Stand

The first thing to buy is a good-quality kart stand. You want a stand that is sturdy, easy to maneuver, and has good-sized wheels and tires. This will help make pushing your kart easier when

Choose a high-quality kart stand with large, pneumatic tires. Working on your kart will be easier and getting to the grid will be less of a hassle.
Sean Buur

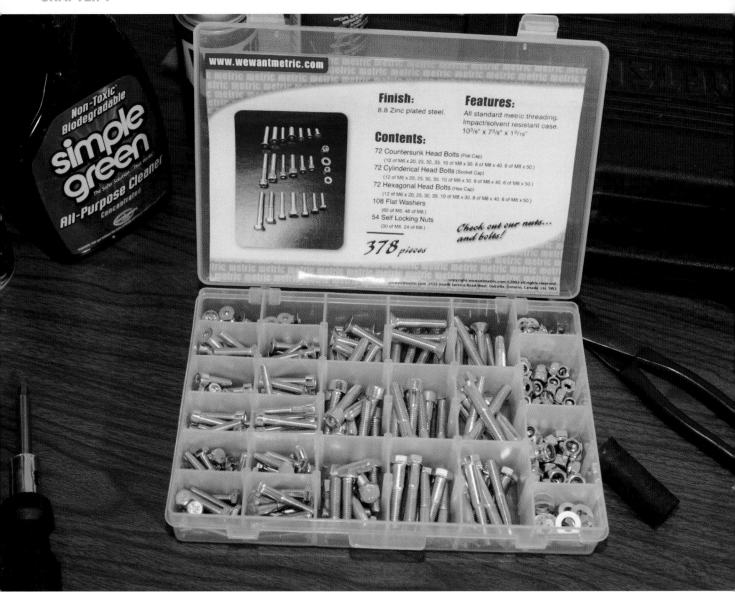

www.wewantmetric.com

Finish:
8.8 Zinc plated steel.

Features:
All standard metric threading.
Impact/solvent resistant case.
10³/₈" x 7³/₈" x 1⁹/₁₆"

Contents:
72 Countersunk Head Bolts (Flat Cap)
(12 of M6 x 20, 25, 30, 35, 10 of M8 x 30, 8 of M8 x 40, 6 of M8 x 50.)
72 Cylinderical Head Bolts (Socket Cap)
(12 of M6 x 20, 25, 30, 35, 10 of M8 x 30, 8 of M8 x 40, 6 of M8 x 50.)
72 Hexagonal Head Bolts (Hex Cap)
(12 of M6 x 20, 25, 30, 35, 10 of M8 x 30, 8 of M8 x 40, 6 of M8 x 50.)
108 Flat Washers
(60 of M6, 48 of M8.)
54 Self Locking Nuts
(30 of M6, 24 of M8.)

Check out our nuts... and bolts!

378 *pieces*

A good selection of the right hardware is a must. Most speedway karts are built in the United States and use SAE (Society of Automotive Engineers) or standard hardware, while most sprint karts are made in Europe and use metric hardware.
Jeff Deskins

Make sure your tools and equipment are in good shape.

rolling it over gravel and asphalt irregularities at the track. You don't want to get frustrated with a bad kart stand before you get to the grid. A range of models is available—from basic units like the ones from RLV, to more enhanced models like the ones from Andersen Pit Karts. Both models feature big pneumatic wheels to run over gravel surfaces and a large lower tray for tools and parts. The RLV unit folds up for storage. The Andersen kart stand can be used to transport the kart. Choose the model that's right for you.

Hand Tools

You will need a good set of hand tools—remember, many karts use metric

hardware. A basic set will include T-handles, nut drivers, sockets, and combination wrenches, along with screwdrivers, hammers, and punches. Make sure your tools and equipment are in good shape. Worn or broken tools will only lead to problems with your kart. It's important that you spend the money to buy a well-known brand of tools. Cheap tools strip and round off nuts and bolts, making maintenance difficult. Try to keep your tools organized so you can locate them easily, saving time and frustration. You will need a few specialty tools that are only available at your local kart shop. They include an air gauge, a brake bleeder, and safety-wire pliers.

Also, you may need a clutch puller if you're running in a clutch class.

Lubes and Oils

Your kart will go through a lot of lubrication. Make sure you have chain lube, bearing lube, and spray-on lube. Having a multipurpose lube like PL50 from Torco is very important. These spray-on lubes are great for repelling water and also for breaking down grease. Be sure to buy high-quality lubes to help ensure long life for your driveline components.

Keeping your kart clean is a must. It's always easier to work on a clean kart than a dirty one. Get your hands on some general-purpose cleaners, like Simple Green®, for degreasing, along with carburetor cleaner and brake cleaner. Never use a water hose to spray your kart clean, as the water will ruin the bearings on your kart. It's much easier to clean your kart while the dirt and grease are fresh. For this reason, I always spend five minutes at the end of a day at the track cleaning my kart before I go home.

Metric Hardware

Make sure you have a full selection of the metric nuts, bolts, and washers you need to keep your kart in shape. Avoid reusing Nylock nuts too often. Nothing is worse than having a breakdown because a 10-cent nut fell off your kart. Go to your local nut-and-bolt supply shop or try www.wewantmetric.com.

There are only a handful of different fasteners on a kart, making a complete inventory easy to keep. A good assortment of the right pieces is critical to keeping your kart in top running shape. Most karts use 8.8 zinc-plated steel metric hardware. Always try to comply with OEM specifications.

Other Stuff

A kart has several items that are best described as consumables and should be replaced on a regular basis as part of an ongoing maintenance schedule. Parts that wear quickly and should be replaced often include: fuel line, fuel filter, water hose, throttle return springs, throttle cable, wheel studs, wheel nuts, spark plugs, and chain. We recommend that you carry spares of all of these items.

TRANSPORTING: GETTING TO THE TRACK

There are a number of ways to get your kart to the track. The important part is to get there safely. The primary choices for getting your kart from home to track are truck, van, or trailer. The key is you don't need a huge truck and a massive trailer to kart race. Most of your karting gear can be boxed in plastic totes. The size and shape of a kart fits well into most standard truck, van, and trailer configurations.

Truck

A pickup truck is a great way to get your kart to the track. The tail gate on your truck alsoworks as a great tool and parts bench at the track. The important thing when using a truck is to get everything tied down properly—including all your gas cans. Try to keep things like your race gear in the cab to be sure it's safe and dry.

Many racers put their kart on a raised platform above the wheelwells and slip all their tools underneath. Strapping the kart down is very important. Old race tires make for great cushions. Put a few of these used tires under the frame before tying down will help to hold the kart in place. If your truck has a shell or cap, this will further protect your kart from the elements during transportation.

Van

With so many minivans on the road today there's a good chance you may own or have access to one. Also, many

Keeping your kart clean is a must.

Parts that wear quickly and should be replaced often include: fuel line, fuel filter, water hose, throttle return springs, throttle cable, wheel studs, wheel nuts, spark plugs, and chain.

Here is a pickup truck loaded for a trip to the track. When you pack properly, you can fit a lot in the back of a pickup. *Jeff Deskins*

places rent commercial-size vans to use for a weekend. With the rear seats out, many karts will fit in nicely. Adding a roof rack or carry bag is great for fuel and oil cans. Do not transport fuel inside your van. Again, you can place your kart on a platform and put your tools underneath. Even though the kart and equipment is inside, be sure to strap it down properly.

Trailer

The nice part about having an enclosed trailer is protecting your kart, tools, and equipment from the elements while traveling. This is especially important for longer hauls where you may encounter rain. While trailers do require storage, you can purchase some very small and compact units that tow very easily behind any vehicle; they're available at hardware centers such as Home Depot. There are some toy haulers that combine living quarters with cargo space, great for those overnight stays. For some great tow tips, go to www.paceamerican.com.

Just remember to be safe and never overload.

TOWING TIPS

With a trailer in tow, you're operating a vehicle combination that is longer, heavier, wider and taller. Make compensating adjustments in your normal driving practices. Here are some helpful trailering tips:

1. Check the trailer's lights, brakes, hitch, etc. so you know they are all working properly.

2. Slow down. Moderate to slower driving speeds put less strain on your tow vehicle and trailer and make for safer traveling.

3. Allow extra time and space between your rig and traffic. You will need both when passing and stopping, especially if your trailer is not equipped with brakes.

4. Check rear view mirrors. Doing this frequently will let you know that your trailer is riding properly. We recommend outside rear view mirrors on both sides of your tow vehicle.

5. Turn wider. You need to make wider turns at curves and corners because your trailer's wheels are generally closer to the inside of a turn than the wheels on your tow vehicle.

6. Pass with extra care and caution. It takes more time and distance to get around slower moving vehicles and into the correct lane when you've got a trailer in tow.

7. Be aware of the wind direction and speed. To avoid swaying, be prepared for sudden changes in air pressure and wind buffering when larger vehicles pass from either direction. Slow down a bit and keep a firm hold on your steering wheel. Aim straight down your lane.

8. Conserve fuel. You'll go farther on a tank of gas at moderate speeds. Higher speeds increase wind resistance against the trailer and reduce fuel mileage.

9. Avoid sudden stops and starts. This can cause skidding, sliding, or jackknifing—even if your trailer has brakes. Avoid quick stops when turning. Smooth, gradual starts and stops will also improve your gas mileage.

10. Signal your intentions. Let surrounding vehicles know what you intended to do well in advance before your stop, turn, change lanes, or pass.

11. Shift to a lower gear. A lower gear will help ease the load on the transmission and engine when going over steep hills, sand, gravel, or dirt roads. If your tow vehicle has an overdrive gear, shifting out of overdrive to a lower gear may improve your gas mileage.

12. Always be courteous. Make it as easy as possible for faster moving vehicles to pass you. Keep to the right of the road and prepare to slow down if passing vehicles need extra time to return to their proper lane.

13. Don't tailgate. Allow at least one car and trailer length between you and the vehicle ahead of you for each 10 miles per hour on your speedometer. Three seconds should be the minimum distance.

14. If a problem occurs, don't panic—stay calm and cool. If you experience a sudden bumping or fishtailing, it may indicate a flat tire. Don't jam on the brakes or mash the accelerator in an attempt to drive out of it. Instead, slowly come to a stop as you keep driving in as straight a line as possible. If conditions permit, coast to a very slow speed and try to avoid braking, except when your wheels are straight ahead and your tow vehicle and trailer are in line with each other.

15. If your trailer begins to fishtail as you accelerate to highway speed, back off the accelerator a bit. This should stop the fishtailing. If it begins again as you increase speed, stop and check your load. It probably isn't distributed evenly from side to side or it is too far back to put a sufficient load on the hitch ball. It is recommended that 10 percent of the trailer load be on the hitch. Redistribute the load as necessity dictates before continuing on the highway.

Remember, never carry passengers in a trailer while moving. Check hub temperature at each stop. Adjust sensitivity of brake controller to match load.

Reprinted with permission of PACE American Trailers. www.paceamerican.com

Chapter 2

KARTING FORMATS

Racers get ready to take to the grid in the RMax Challenge, a series that uses the ROTAX Touch and Go engine. Drivers from over 72 countries race to crown a world champion. *Sean Buur*

Each format is very specific for the types of chassis and engine combinations that are used.

Karting has many different formats that cover a lot of different age ranges. At first it can seem a bit confusing and a little overwhelming, but once you begin to understand the differences you can find the right form of karting for you. It's important that you take some time and understand all the formats before you decide where to begin.

There are several important factors to consider before you choose your karting format. Some people want to ease into the sport, while others want to jump right in. First, consider age. For example, young children need to start in a class and format where they can learn the basics. The next consideration is budget. Set a reasonable budget that you know you can afford. Don't get into a kart that's

expensive to operate and maintain if you don't have the time or resources. Finally, be sure to set clear expectations and goals. Understand what you want to achieve in your racing.

KARTING FORMATS

Karts come in many different sizes and take many forms. Each format is very specific for the types of chassis and engine combinations that are used. After researching kart tracks in your area, the next step is to attend a race weekend event. Every region has classes that are more popular than others; it's always more fun to compete in a class that has a lot of drivers. Not only will the competition be better, but there will be more people to help you if you have questions or problems.

Indoor

Indoor karting is one of the most popular forms of karting in the world. The biggest benefit of indoor karting is that it is more accessible in urban areas and can operate year round. This is especially important in northern climates that have a short summer racing season. In most cases the karts are provided, so all you require is a need for speed. Most indoor karting facilities offer a pay-per-lap program, which allows you to run the number of laps you want. Many indoor facilities also have race nights where you can experi-

ence practice, qualifying, and racing. Because many new drivers' first laps are in an indoor kart, the karts are very heavy and are built to withstand heavy abuse. For safety, most indoor karts have full wraparound body kits that keep tires from locking together in the event of contact with another kart. Indoor tracks are very tight and are usually lined on both sides with some type of safety barrier. The racing surface is typically concrete, which makes traction hard to find.

Indoor karting can be a great place to hone your driving skills and develop

F1 Boston, located just outside of Boston, MA is one of the top indoor karting facilities in the North America. Drivers are treated to a bright, clean and fun environment. Equipment includes helmets, neck collars and coveralls. *photo F1Boston*

Many indoor facilities also have race nights where you can experience practice, qualifying, and racing.

Arrive and Drive programs offer close and competitive karting at an affordable price. These programs can help you get a feel for the sport before you buy into it. *Sean Buur*

Arrive and drive programs are a great place to learn karting without having to buy a kart or keep up with maintenance.

your interest in karting. Some indoor karting facilities run regular leagues in addition to the lap rental programs. One of the largest and most unique facilities is F1 Boston located in Braintree, Massachusetts.

Arrive and Drive

There are many outdoor tracks, driving schools, and kart shops that offer arrive and drive programs. Arrive and drive programs are a great place to learn

karting without having to buy a kart or keep up with maintenance. The track or shop provides the kart chassis, engine, and all the equipment required to race. You show up and sign in for a day of driving, and the track will fit you to a kart and get you ready to race. You can start by renting the kart for practice, then as you feel more comfortable and your skills get better, you can drive in an actual race. Some Arrive and drive programs are based on a league format.

Spec Touch and Go Classes

There are a number of new karting classes that are targeted to the karting newcomer. One of the newest is the 'spec' electric start, or touch-and-go, classes. Spec refers to the fact that one manufacturer designs all of the components for that kart. The kart is developed and sold as a complete package, requiring no additional assembly or parts, right down to the tires. This makes purchasing the kart and maintaining it easier for the karting newcomer. The goal is to support the grassroots racer and establish an environment with emphasis on driver skill.

There are a number of benefits from running and racing in a spec class. First, you race against identical karts, so it really becomes a race of drivers. As a driver you can focus your time and energies to race craft and race techniques. Also, the rules are created to keep the karts equal using sealed

Robert Wickens, Formula BMW driver and top Canadian kart racer paces the F1K senior kart at the Cameron Motorsports Karting Complex in Hamilton, Ontario, Canada. *Teresa Matkovich*

engines and specified parts, keeping chassis changes to a minimum. In many cases the gearing and jetting is set each race day to make racing even easier. The need for expensive engine builds and a huge selection of components is not required. The focus and emphasis of the program is head to head competition.

One of the newest is the F1K program developed by Cameron Motorsports of Hamilton, Ontario and CRG of Italy. The F1K kart uses a

CRG chassis along with a Maxter kart-racing engine. The air-cooled engine has electric start and uses a centrifugal single gear clutch. The on-board battery is self-charging from the magneto, making for long battery life and easy operation. This program is available with 60cc and 125cc models. The 60cc cadet model uses a standard 35-inch (900-mm) wheelbase chassis. The 125cc model uses a 42-inch (1,030-mm) chassis and can be operated as a junior or senior model.

For the junior model the ignition is restricted, capping the maximum rpms at 14,000. This reduces the horsepower to 20. The senior model has a maximum power output of 30 horsepower at 16,000 rpm.

Other similar classes include the Easykart program from Birel and the Vortex program from Tony Kart. Spec programs are great forms of karting for newcomers or for drivers who have less time to spend on tuning. Be sure to find out if your local kart track offers such programs.

The F1K kart is built to 2005 CIK standards and uses the latest bodywork and components. The onboard electric start eliminates the need for a hand held starter. *Teresa Matkovich*

Here drivers run in a two-stroke oval series popular in California. Speedway karting is known for close, fast racing and tough competition. *Sean Buur*

Sprint racing takes place year round in most areas, in dry and wet conditions.

You pay to join the league and have the opportunity to race on a weekly basis. Drivers are divided into weight categories to keep the competition close.

Arrive and drive programs are a great way to test your skills, learn more about the sport, and really understand what is right for you before you make a purchase. One of the largest and most established arrive and drive programs is the Canadian Rookie Karting Championship located at the Cameron Motorsports Karting Complex in Hamilton, Ontario. This program has been in operation for over 10 years and has more than 1,000 members racing seven days a week. Many drivers have been participating for years, while others use this series as a step to a sprint karting program. Check your local track or shop to see if Arrive and drive programs are offered in your area.

Sprint

Sprint karting is the most popular form of karting in the world and the format most closely associated with karting. Fields can be as big as 35 karts and use a rolling start to begin each race. Races usually last between 10 and 20 minutes, with a predetermined number of laps. Sprint racing takes place year round in most areas, in dry and wet conditions. This kind of kart racing utilizes smaller, paved road courses (sprint tracks), with left and right turns, gener-

ally about 1 mile in length, with kerbing to help mark the inside and out of the driving line. Sprint karts are also raced in large street races—tracks set up in shopping-center parking lots or on city streets. Some street races are very successful; the Rock Island Grand Prix in Illinois draws over 20,000 spectators every year!

Sprint karts are of the sit-up variety and use specially built chassis designed to turn both left and right. Engines are both four cycle and two cycle in a wide variety of types, including gearbox. Two-stroke engines can operate as direct-drive and as clutch-driven karts, while all four-cycle karts are clutch driven.

Speedway

Speedway kart racing is the most popular form of karting in the United States and is concentrated on the East Coast. This form of karting is most closely associated with stock-car racing. The racing is done on oval tracks, running counterclockwise. These tracks are very short and have dirt, asphalt, and concrete surfaces.

Dirt tracks are extremely popular throughout the United States and range from tracks that are flat to steeply banked; they vary from 1/10 mile to 1/4 mile in length. The surface can be loose soft dirt or hard-packed clay, which is usually wet to start and dries throughout the race.

Asphalt tracks are also very popular but are not as numerous as dirt tracks. Asphalt tracks range from little bull rings to wide-open 1/2-mile or longer stock-car tracks with steep banking. Karts are set up to work with left-only turns so the chassis is offset to the left, helping the

Speedway kart racing is by far the largest segment of karting in North America. Here drivers are running Speedway karts on a paved or asphalt track. *Rowdy Jordan*

Speedway tracks are very short and can have dirt, asphalt, and concrete surfaces.

Arrive and drive programs offer great racing. Here drivers in the Canadian Rookie Karting Challenge compete in the finals. Over 1,200 racers compete for the top prize. *Teresa Matkovich*

kart turn one way very easily. Speedway karts stand out with their large front bodywork and long side panels, which are necessary due to the close proximity of the karts while racing. The karts are primarily four cycle, using the Briggs & Stratton flathead engine. The use of overhead valve (OHV) engines is becoming more popular, and in many areas, these karts run on methanol instead of gasoline. Drivers spend a lot of time choosing the right tires to help them get traction on slippery dirt and ever-changing surfaces. The karts also run with stagger in the front and rear tires, with the right-side tires being larger than the left-side tires. This helps increase the kart's ability to turn left.

Enduro or Road Race

Enduro, or road racing, is a form of kart racing on large road-racing courses (e.g., Road America or Laguna Seca). Typically, special enduro karts are used for this type of racing, with the lie-down enduros looking the most dramatic. Because the tracks are so large, straight-away speed and low drag are key to fast lap times. The lay-down kart drivers literally lie on their backs in the kart, with only their heads up to see where to drive. Obviously, the setup is very different and speeds tend to be quite a bit higher. Enduro racing is usually more expensive than sprint racing, and is not often recommended for beginners. There is also sit-up enduro racing,

In Speedway racing, it is common to see racers drive three wide as they work to pass drivers. "Carry your speed" is especially important in speedway racing on paved tracks. There is little room for error. *Rowdy Jordan*

Enduro racing can be fun and has a loyal following.

Racers in the Laydown or Enduro class run on large tracks such as the famous Daytona International Speedway. Speeds can reach 125 miles per hour, Drivers need a great deal or experience to drive these karts. ***Todd McCall***

in which ordinary sprint karts are used, but with a larger fuel tank. Enduro races typically don't last a fixed number of laps, but rather a predetermined length of 30 to 45 minutes. Enduro racing can be fun and has a loyal following. However, the biggest drawback to Enduro racing is the lack of track avail-

ability, and the expense of track time. Because most tracks are designed for car racing, the schedule is often booked and renting and driving on Enduro tracks costs much more than other karting formats.

Vintage

Vintage racing is an extremely popular karing format, with it's racing being more based on the karts, *not* on intense competition. As we discussed earlier, karting has a long history. Many of those original pioneers are pulling their old karts out of the back of the garage and restoring them to their original glory. Vintage karting is a great way to look back at the past and enjoy the early days of the sport. The Vintage Kart Olympics attract many old karters and have been held in the Midwest in the past. The disadvantage of vintage racing is constant tuning and maintenance, due to the karts being old. For this reason, vintage racing is not recommended for karting newcomers.

KARTING BREAKDOWNS

In each category of karting, races are divided into several different classes. These classes are generally separated by age, kart weight, and engine type. Another popular way to separate classes is by using a restrictor plate, which sits between the carburetor and the engine intake. In some two-stroke classes, different exhaust mufflers are used to separate classes. The idea is to reduce

Drivers running on oval tracks will "draft" the kart in front them by staying close behind and right on their bumper. When drafting, the second kart to experience less wind resistance and can pass the kart in front more easily. *Rowdy Jordan*

the horsepower for younger drivers. As they move up, you can put in a bigger restrictor plate and increase power.

Every class has a minimum weight requirement, that way drivers of different sizes and weights can be competitive with each other. Class weights are taken with kart *and* driver as the drivers exit the track from a race. It can be surprising how just a small weight difference makes a big lap time difference. All karts must meet a minimum class weight or face disqualification.

CLASSES

Kid kart classes include competitors between 5 and 7 years old, and use purpose-built karting chassis with a special 50-cc Comer C-51 engine. The spirit and intent of this class is to allow kids to get accustomed to driving a kart and driving with other competitors on a track. Most clubs offer this class for exhibition only, with all competitors receiving the same trophy.

Junior sportsman or cadet classes are offered for kids ages 8 to 12. In these classes, the engines range from stock 5-horsepower Briggs to 60-cc Shifters to Yamaha Junior Sportsman Can engines. Kids in this class run in the turquoise or purple restrictor-plate classes. Check into local rules and the availability of classes before deciding on a package.

Junior classes are open to kids 12 to 15 years old, and are faster than the

Racing is great for drivers and speed junkies of all ages. Racing offers a safe, fun, and well-organized environment to enjoy a day of outdoor activity. Here a group of Masters, or over 35 drivers, take to the track. *Teresa Matkovich*

Class weights are taken with kart and driver as the drivers exit the track from a race.

Dylan Nobile of California runs at the head of the pack driving a Nevoso kart. The HPV class is one of the largest and most popular classes of junior sprint kart racing. A great place to learn your racing craft, all drivers in the Comer class run the same 80cc clutch-driven engine on cadet-size frames. *Sean Buur*

There are usually a lot of senior classes offered in every region.

cadet and rookie classes—some classes are as fast as the senior classes—because even though the power is less than senior classes, the light weight helps the karts corner fast. Classes can range from Yamaha Junior Can to 80-cc Shifters to Briggs Junior Restricted. Check local rules and classes offered in your area.

Senior classes are for drivers 15 and older. They are offered in a wide range of classes including a masters class at some tracks for drivers 35 and older. There are usually a lot of senior classes offered in every region, from Yamaha Pipe classes that put out 18 to 20 horsepower, to the restricted Yamaha Can classes producing 12 to 14 horsepower, to Shifter Kart and ICC

Shifter engines with front-wheel brakes. Senior classes are also broken down by weight and engine package. A popular entry-level class is the blueprinted Stock Briggs classes. Using the same motor, there are subclasses, such as Briggs Stock Light and Briggs Stock Heavy. Again, this allows drivers that weigh more to not have a disadvantage against drivers who weigh less. Classes are also available that use the new Briggs Animal engine, as well as the Briggs Unlimited and Open classes. Other popular classes at some tracks are the Yamaha two-cycle classes or two-cycle Unlimited classes. One of the newest formats of karting is Touch and Go (TAG). Different classes are popular at different tracks, so be sure to find out what's popular in your area.

UNDERSTANDING THE RULES
Pretech for Safety

One very important area of karting, regardless of the class you race is the prerace technical inspection. The purpose of this inspection is to verify that your kart is race ready and meets the set standards for safety compliance. All karts registered to race in the event must pass through the safety inspection. Most tracks have a designated area where drivers line up and a tech inspector will go over your kart. You must usually present a form that indicates the class, engine, number, and driver of the kart.

The inspector checks for elements that could cause problems. They look for cracks in the frame, proper body-work, secure weights, and no protruding bars or exhaust parts. Most tracks will also ask to see your helmet to confirm that it meets the required standards. An inspector may ask you make certain repairs or changes and then return to tech for reinspection.

Prior to the start of qualifying, the karts are "painted," or sealed. This includes marking tires and certain engine pieces. The tech inspector will place a dab of paint or tech seal on bolts and nuts on components like the carburetor, head, exhaust, and side case. This is to ensure that the kart racer doesn't change any parts of his kart from qualifying to the final.

Drivers' Meeting

The drivers' meeting is an important, and in most cases, mandatory part of the race day. The drivers meetings are for

An inspector may ask you make certain repairs or changes and then return to tech for reinspection.

Kart racing takes focus and discipline. Here Garett Grist concentrates on his racing line during Comer Cadet action during the World Karting Association George Kugler Manufacturers Cup Race in South Bend, Indiana. *Sean Buur*

Sometimes the most important moments in karting happen after the race, when drivers and parents get a chance to celebrate victories and learn from defeats. *Sean Buur*

Drivers should ask all questions and express any safety concerns while at the driver's meeting.

both drivers and race officials to review the schedule of events, highlight the critical safety rules, and address any unique procedures for the day. The driver's meeting usually takes place after practice and before the race begins. Race officials, such as the race director or race steward, will review the start procedures and the tech procedures.

Drivers should ask all questions and express any safety concerns while at the driver's meeting; many times, new drivers to the club will be welcomed during the meeting. These meetings should be attended by the parents of young drivers to ensure the message is delivered.

Post tech for Rules Application

After every final race, the top three to five karts will be placed in an impound area for technical inspection. Inspectors will first check to see if any paint or tech seals have been broken, indicating that a part may have been changed. The inspectors are most interested in the engine. They'll check the engine serial number to confirm it matches the number on the tech sheet the driver filled out prior to pretech inspection. They'll pull the engine apart to ensure that all internal parts meet the technical standards published in the rule book. They may also check the size of the carburetor and the volume of the cylinder head.

Top-flight champion drivers get tuning support from professional kart racing mechanics. These drivers develop the on- and off-track skills required to move into car racing.
Sean Buur

Chapter 3

ENGINE FORMATS

The Briggs & Stratton Animal is quickly becoming the engine of choice for speedway karting through out the United States. This OHV four-cycle engine is replacing the older Briggs flathead engines. *Sean Buur*

The biggest difference between a two-cycle and a four-cycle engine is in the torque output.

Karting makes use of both four-stroke and two-stroke engines across the various kart racing formats we discussed earlier. Aside from the distinct differences between the two types of engines, how the engines are produced is very different as well. Most four-stroke karting engines are built from common utility engines found on many different power equipment applications. Two-stroke engines, on the other hand, are purpose-built racing engines designed specifically for karting.

On a four-cycle engine, four piston strokes up and down inside the cylinder complete a power cycle. This means that it takes two crank revolutions, or 720 degrees, to complete a power cycle, unlike two-cycle engines, which only require two strokes—one revolution of

the crankshaft—to complete a power cycle. Is one better than the other? Like the answer to many questions in karting, that depends. Traditionally, two-stroke engines do produce more horsepower, but at a cost. They consume more fuel, require more maintenance, and are subject to expensive failures. Four-cycle engines, on the other hand, produce less horsepower, but are more reliable and are usually easier to maintain.

The biggest difference between a two-cycle and a four-cycle engine is in the torque output, which is the power produced at the initial rotation of the crankshaft in the lower or initial rpm levels. Four-cycle engines produce considerably more torque, which means they can accelerate more quickly and build speed faster than two-cycles.

As the rpm level rises, and the two-stroke power really kicks in, the engine begins to pull. So, depending on the application and the track conditions, either engine can be a potent powerplant.

FOUR-CYCLE 101
Overview
This section will focus on the basics of four-cycle kart racing engines. The engines all have one thing in common: each is based on a mass-production utility or commercial unit. These utility engines are designed for long life and low maintenance, making them perfect for karting. Because they are mass produced, the cost of production and development is very low, providing karters with a cost-effective starting point. In order to make these engines race ready, a number of changes and modifications are necessary. In some cases, these changes are made at the factory; in other cases your local engine builder will do the work.

Four-cycle engine technology has been evolving very quickly because of two different forces. First, the advances made in car racing continue to push the envelope of what four-cycle engines can achieve. Some race car rpm levels reach 20,000, a level that was previously thought to be impossible. Second, the move to ban two-cycle engines globally because of significant environmental impact has forced major engine manufacturers to spend millions of dollars on research and development to perfect small, light, and reliable four-cycle engines. As the major brand manufacturers like Briggs & Stratton, Yamaha, and Honda continue to strive for greater reliability and efficiency in these engines, karting has greatly benefited.

Let's start by discussing the parts in a four-cycle motor. The block is comprised of the crankcase and cylinder, and is made of a light alloy like aluminum. The cylinder is an integrated part of the block, unlike a two-cycle, which has a removable cylinder. In some engines, the cylinder—sometimes called the barrel—uses a very durable steel sleeve. The left, or power take-off (PTO), side of the engine has a removable cover to allow for engine servicing.

The cylinder head sits on top of the cylinder and accommodates the spark plug. The shape of the cylinder head helps determine the volume of the combustion chamber, which varies from motor to motor depending on power requirements. Because the cylinder, head is subjected to so much heat, it is a major area for some type of cooling. Running inside the cylinder, the piston is made of light alloy, with three rings at the top that run along the cylinder walls. The top ring seals in compression for maximum power, and

In a four-stroke engine, the piston moves up to TDC and pushes the exhaust gas out through the exhaust valve. The red area shows where the exhaust gas travels. *Sean Buur*

Four-cycle engines are designed for long life and low maintenance.

The camshaft uses two different elements to function: lift and duration.

The camshaft of a four-stroke engine, painted blue here, is turned by the crankshaft and moves the valvetrain. The camshaft is the heart of a four-stroke engine. *Sean Buur*

the bottom ring seals the oil in the crankcase for maximum lubrication. The middle ring is called the scraper ring and removes any excess oil or deposits from the cylinder walls. The top of the piston, the cylinder head, and the cylinder barrel combine to create the combustion chamber.

The connecting rod connects the piston to the crankshaft and delivers power from the combustion chamber to the drive system. It is generally made from forged steel, but in some cases it's machined from billet aluminum. It needs to be extremely strong to take the shock of the inertia at top dead center (TDC) and at bottom dead center (BDC). In these utility-based engines, there are no separate bearings used to mount the bottom of the connecting rod

to the crankshaft, or the top of the connecting rod to the piston wrist pin. The relatively low rpm levels do not require a special bearing like you would see in a two-cycle engine. The crankshaft machined to fit bearings at each end. The center is offset to allow the crankshaft to rotate as the piston moves the connecting rod up and down.

The heart and soul of a four-cycle engine is the camshaft. Other factors such as piston shape, combustion chamber, carburetion, and valve size are critical, but the camshaft is key. The camshaft uses two different elements to function: lift and duration. Lift is the amount the valve opens, which determines the size of the opening through which fuel flows in or exhaust flows out. Duration is the time that the valve stays open during the cycle, which determines the amount of fuel that can flow in or exhaust gas that can flow out.

The key is to find the correct balance of lift and duration during the power cycle to maximize power output. The duration and lift are built into the camshaft lobes, the machined surfaces of the camshaft that the valve lifters sit on. The oblong or elliptical shape of the lobes will move the lifters up and down, opening and closing the valves as the camshaft turns with the crankshaft.

The ignition delivers the spark that starts the combustion. In most cases, a four-cycle engine does not require a battery to operate and can produce enough of its own electrical charge. The initial electrical pulse comes from the magneto. The magneto meters and coordinates the delivery of the pulse. The magneto then amplifies the charge to the voltage level required to jump the spark plug gap and ignite the fuel/air mixture.

Here is the sequence that operates a four-cycle engine. Let's start at top dead center (TDC), which means the piston is at the very top of the cylinder.

From TDC, the piston falls and the intake valve opens, pulling a fuel and air mixture from the carburetor into the cylinder. As the piston hits bottom dead center (BDC), the intake valve closes. The piston then moves back up the cylinder, compressing the fuel in the combustion chamber. Near TDC the spark plug fires, exploding the fuel. The piston is driven down on what's called the power stroke. At BDC, the exhaust valve opens as the piston begins to move up the cylinder. On this fourth and final stroke, the exhaust gas is pushed out through the exhaust port. As the piston reaches TDC, the exhaust valve closes and the intake valve opens to begin the cycle all over again.

COOLING

Karting engines, both two- and four-cycle, can be cooled in two different ways: air cooled and water cooled. Regardless of how the engine is cooled, the area that needs the most cooling is the cylinder. This is where the explosion of air/fuel mixture in the combustion chamber creates the heat.

Air-cooled engines, as the name implies, are cooled using air passing by the engine. These engines use large radial fins that pull the heat away from the cylinder. As the kart travels down the track the air rushing by pulls the heat away from these fins and helps keep the engine operating temperature lower.

Water-cooled engines use a cooling system that surrounds the cylinder heat with water that is circulated through a radiator. The water pulls heat away from the cylinder and cylinder head and flows to the radiator. The radiator, just like in your kart, pulls heat out of the water and returns it to the cylinder. Notice we use the term *water, not liquid*. The use of oil-based coolants is not allowed in karting, because if leaked on the track surface, it becomes dangerously slipppery. Most engine manufacturers recommend using distilled water.

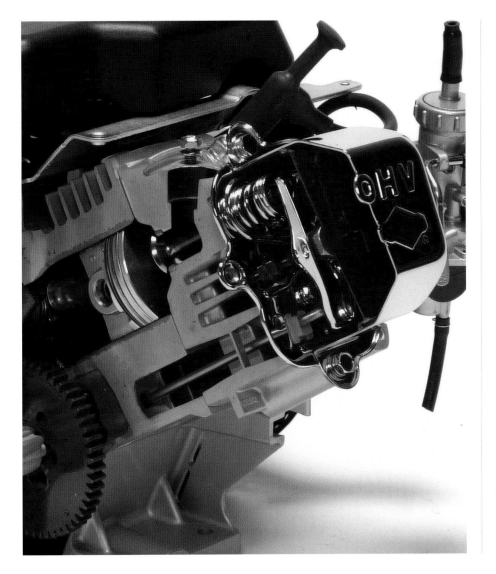

The valvetrain of a four-stroke includes the lifters, rocker arms, valve springs, and valves. Most karting four-stroke engines are a single-cylinder design with one exhaust valve and one intake valve. *Sean Buur*

All moving parts in a four-cycle engine require lubrication to function properly.

WHAT OIL CAN TELL YOU

The oil in the crankcase can tell you a lot about your engine. One thing to look for in used oil is particles of metal coming from bearings, or rubber coming from seals that are ready to fail. Also, oil that is very black can indicate carbon buildup, while oil with gas deposits can show fuel leaking. Water in the engine shows up as a milky white residue in the oil. Be sure to change the oil often and try to keep an eye on oil levels. A good rule of thumb is to change the oil at the end of every race day. Most engines require about 16 ounces (500 to 600 ml) of oil. Be sure to check with your engine builder for the proper amount. In some cases, you may choose to run with less than the manufacturer's recommended amount to allow the crankshaft to spin more freely, but then you run the risk of not having enough oil and damaging your engine.

All moving parts in a four-cycle engine require lubrication to function properly. To accomplish this, oil is held in the crankcase to lubricate the crankshaft, camshaft, connecting rod bearing, piston pin bearing, cylinder walls, and valvetrain. Most engines will use basic 30- or 40-weight oil, like 10W/30 or 15W/40. There are special racing oils for four-cycle engines, which are very thin, since these engines don't use an oil pump. Crankcase oil is moved around to all the vital parts by a dipper, which is mounted to the bottom of the connecting rod. As the crank spins, the dipper splashes oil around inside the crankcase and to all the other parts that need to be lubricated. Besides lubricating, the oil collects any impurities, contaminants, or particles that may be inside the crankcase.

A close up of the filler cap for a typical four-cycle engine. This plug cap needs only be finger tight and should be checked regularly. Be sure to replace this cap before the engine is restarted. *Sean Buur*

Four-cycle racing engines can run on both gasoline and methanol. Both have advantages and disadvantages. Gasoline is easy to purchase and handle, and the many additives used today will help extend the life of the engine. Running higher-octane levels or using unleaded race gasoline has no value in small-displacement four-cycle engines. Premium pump gas is great. The down side to gasoline is a relatively low combustion temperature, which, if handled improperly, can lead to injury. A gasoline fire must be put out with a gasoline-rated fire extinguisher.

Methanol is great because it runs cooler, while creating greater combustion when ignited. Also, methanol has a much higher flash point, so there is less risk of fire. The downside is that a methanol flame cannot be seen; it is virtually invisible. It can, however, be put out with water. Also, methanol has no protective additives, so engine parts are subject to premature wear. Another problem with methanol is that it absorbs moisture and must be handled very carefully to ensure that it doesn't become contaminated. Before you make any fuel changes, check with your engine builder and local track to see what fuels are allowed.

Briggs Raptor 3

The foundation of four-cycle sprint racing, the Briggs, has been a workhorse for over 40 years. This engine was first put into service in the very early days of karting because it was compact, lightweight, and readily available. What is unique about this engine is the use of a side valve system. The exhaust and intake valves operate vertically, directly behind the cylinder wall. They run directly off the camshaft and open upward. The carburetor has a built-in pump and the fuel tank is mounted directly to the bottom of the carburetor. No longer in production at Briggs & Stratton Company, this engine is being phased out by most sprint racing organizations, but continues to be the engine of choice for Speedway karting.

In all racing applications, the flathead goes through a significant process such as a general blueprinting, to get it race ready. For the most part, the flathead is run as a stock engine in sprint racing. Some regions and clubs run

Four-cycle racing engines can run on both gasoline and methanol.

Speedway karts that run on dirt-surfaced tracks need to be very clean. After each race drivers wash the dirt and mud off the kart and tires. Allowing the dirt to build up will affect the handling of the kart.
Rowdy Jordan

A Briggs flathead Raptor mounted on a sprint kart at the Rock Island Grand Prix. The side-valve, flathead Briggs Raptor has been part of karting for many years. *Sean Buur*

The World Formula program uses a rev limiter to monitor the maximum allowable engine speed.

modified classes, but even in most stock classes, an aftermarket billet connecting rod can be used, since this is the weak part of this engine. With respect to stock, this means running only OEM parts.

World Formula

The idea of a World Formula engine program began at the top of karting with the CIK/FIA setting the rules and guidelines for introduction of this program to the worldwide karting community. By creating a World Formula engine program, karting can accomplish two things at the same time: move forward into the future and give racing bodies around the world a local class option. With this type of racing program, the engine is less of a factor, making chassis setup and driver skill more important.

To grow karting globally, the World Formula engine program helps to introduce karting into countries that don't have a racing infrastructure. Many developing nations know and love racing but don't have the economic base to ignite the sport at the local level. Currently, 22 countries have a World Formula national class. These include

European countries like Italy and Poland and Pacific Rim countries like India. Also, the World Formula program is making inroads into China. ASN Canada currently has national, regional, and club programs using the World Formula platform with great success. In the United States, this program is proving popular at clubs looking for an entry-level program that provides fun, close racing.

One very unique element of the World Formula program is the use of a rev limiter to monitor the maximum allowable engine speed. Use of a rev limiter is very common in all forms of car racing. The purpose of a rev limiter is to limit the number of revolutions per minute the engine can make by cutting the ignition when the preset maximum level is reached. Just as on race cars, the kart rev limiter is used to maintain longer engine life and to limit power output. Raising or lowering the maximum allowable rpm level allows the same engines to be used for different classes based on age and experience.

The World Formula engine package is complete, including ignition, clutch, carburetor, and exhaust header.

The World Formula engine produced by Briggs & Stratton is the first of its kind, built to a world standard for performance in four-stroke karting engines. This engine is sold as a complete racing package. *Sean Buur*

The Briggs World Formula even comes with an environmentally friendly air filter and an electric starter. All that's required is an engine mount, throttle cable, and fuel line. Everything else you need is included in the kit. Special racing features include barrel-faced domed piston, chrome-faced top ring, billet aluminum rod, dual valve springs, and three-piece automotive-style keepers. The camshaft is specially treated for long life using a Stelite finish, and is ground to exact specifications. Also, the Briggs World Formula uses a cast-aluminum manifold with a rubber carburetor-mounting flange and a racing-designed combustion chamber with a CNC-

Author Jeff Grist paces a Trackmagic Dragon sprint kart powered by a Briggs World Formula engine. This engine is now raced in over 25 countries around the world, including Canada and the United States. *Sean Buur*

The YF200R1 has been designed to maximize the potential of a utility engine.

machined D-shape intake port for maximum performance.

Using the electric starter is optional. If the electric starter motor is removed, a protective metal plate must be installed to cover the opening in the engine shroud left by the removed starter. The installation of a battery is optional. If a battery is used it must not be a wet lead-acid battery. Only dry or gel cell batteries (sealed lead batteries) are permitted.

The World Formula comes with a Premier drum clutch and a quick-change sprocket set (16–17 tooth). The clutch should be mounted outboard, with the sprocket gear on the outside. The sprocket on the clutch can be a No. 35 chain or a No. 219 chain. The clutch should be checked and maintained regularly. Clean out and dust using brake cleaner. Remove any shiny spots on the shoes or drum using medium-coarse sandpaper.

The Green air filter is designed to be environmentally friendly and can be recharged for longer life. If properly maintained, there should be no need for a pre-filter cover.

The only eligible exhaust and muffler for Canada and the United States is the RLV World Formula muffler kit. The kit consists of an RLV muffler, an inner pipe, and two springs. Two different mufflers or silencers are available. Be sure to check with your local sanctioning body to be sure which is the right one for your area. The exhaust system header that comes with the World Formula kit has a built-in support bracket. It attaches to the block using a self-tapping bolt, which is included in the kit. You can tap the hole and use a stud or set screw. This is a nontech item.

We recommend that the engine mount be a flat or very low angle mount. This is because the slide-style carburetor uses floats in the fuel bowl to meter the amount of fuel flowing into the carburetor. If the World Formula has too much slant it can be very difficult to set the proper float height. The Burris Racing 5-degree motor mount works great for this application.

Yamaha YF200R1

The YF200R1 has been in the development and planning process since 2003 and shows great promise in both power and reliability. Yamaha is a world leader in small-displacement high-performance two- and four-cycle engines. This same quality and engineering expertise carries over into everything they build, including aerospace-quality castings for the dual-ball-bearing block, big-valve cylinder head and side cover, and forged, induction-hardened crankshaft.

The YF200R1 engine is derived from the Yamaha MZ175, a small-block utility workhorse used on generators, pumps, and other power equipment. The MZ175 is designed to be very reliable and take a real beating, so it's a great base engine to build upon. Much of 2003 was spent developing the YF200R1, resulting in a racing engine that behaves very well and has lots of power, especially bottom-end torque. Initial tests have set several track records and beat some KT100 Super Box times.

The YF200R1 has been designed to maximize the potential of a utility engine. Using a 10:1 compression ratio, the assigned horsepower range of 16 to 18, makes it a very powerful engine for karting. The peak rpm for an unrestricted senior engine is 7,800 to 7,900. With heavier valve springs installed, the engine is capable of over revs into the 8,000 rpm range. However, early tests have shown no appreciable increase in horsepower at that rpm level. The restricted Junior III engine will peak at 6,700 to 6,900 rpm, making it easy for young racers to drive.

The clutch stall speed should be set at about 4,500 rpm to match the expected torque curve output. Because this engine only runs on pump gas, carbon buildup is not a major issue.

The YF200R1 comes as a kit with all the pieces you need. All you have to do to have a race-ready engine is hone and fit the piston and do some minor grinding in the cylinder head to match the port runners to the valve bowls and intake manifold. No other machining or processing is necessary. Although considered basic engine work, you still want to make sure the work is done right. This is where your engine builder comes into play, helping to complete the work properly from the start. From there, the YF200R1 can be assembled in a short period of time using conventional hand tools. This assembly process is a good guide for all the OHV engines used in the F200 program. Use it as a guideline for engine prep and rebuild. Before completing any major work on your engine, be sure to read the operator's manual carefully. Understand that converting an engine to race specifications will void any kind of warranty. Be sure to talk to your engine builder and get his advice.

One cool thing that's offered for the YF200R1 is an assembly tool kit, which includes all the specialty pieces you need to properly assemble the engine. Possible component damage can happen during assembly without the proper tools. All of these tools can be used on other OHV

The YF200R1 is a new karting program from Yamaha developed by Mike Burris of Burris Racing, of Huntington Beach, California. The engine is designed primarily as a speedway engine, but has crossed over into the sprint kart market.
Sean Buur

engines, so it's a great investment. The kit includes a torque plate, dowel remover (8mm and 10mm), seal-installer side cover, seal-installer block, piston installer, and 6mm and 8mm stud installers.

Currently, there is a good selection of well-known high-performance aftermarket parts companies, including Cometic Gaskets, Wiseco Pistons, Dyno Cams, K&N Filters, LA Sleeves, NGK Spark Plugs, and Tillotson Carburetors. Each company has developed their products based on the F200 specifications and the MZ175 profile. This provides a package that will bring the engine up to maximum specs (displacement, compression ratio, valve size, etc.) and should produce the maximum horsepower out of the box.

TWO-CYCLE 101

Overview

The two-cycle, or two-stroke, engine is truly an amazing engineering marvel because it can produce tremendous horsepower given its compact and simple design. Carburetion and exhaust are key components that need to work together to maximize the engine's output. Three key principles dictate how much power is delivered: engine temperature, power band, and air density.

Basically, a two-stroke operates by compressing a mixture of fuel and air in the combustion chamber. The fuel is a combination of gasoline and oil, premixed to the required specifications. The air/fuel mixture moves through the engine by making use of the high and low pressures created by the piston moving up and down. During the downward path of the piston, known as the power and exhaust stroke, the air/fuel mixture in the crankcase is compressed and forced through the transfer ports up into the combustion chamber.

There are two types of two-stroke engines: reed valve and piston port. On the first type, reed valves are used to control the flow of the air/fuel mixture into the engine. The reed valve is a flap that opens when the crankcase pressure is below atmospheric pressure and closes when crankcase pressure is above atmospheric pressure. ICC, ICA, and ROTAX engines use the reed valve system. The piston port type relies on the size of the port and the timing of the piston to close the intake port at the right time. The Yamaha KT100ES and the Horstman HPV use the piston-port configuration.

Components of a two-cycle engine unclude the cylinder, sometimes called the barrel, is made of a light alloy, like

One neat feature of the YF200R1 program is a complete engine assembly toolkit, which includes everything you need to assemble your engine properly. *Sean Buur*

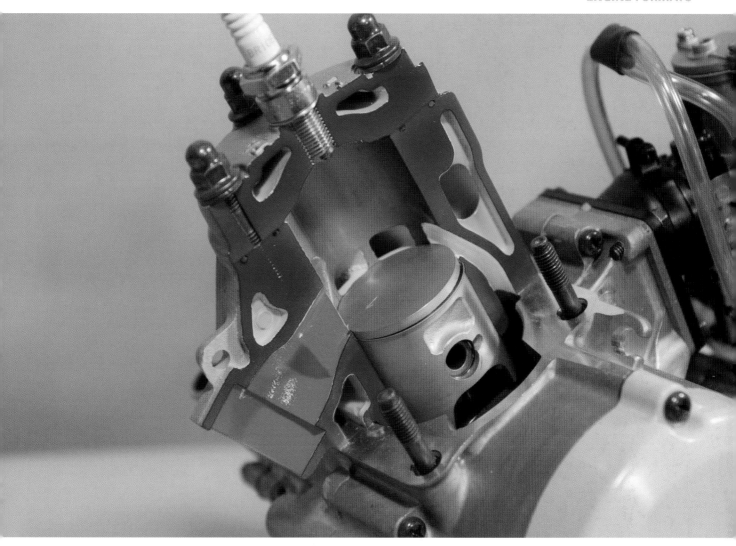

aluminum. Some engines have a very durable steel sleeve or plating called Nikasil. The cylinder has transfer ports cast into it, which allow the air/fuel mixture to flow from the carburetor, through the crankcase, to the combustion chamber. The cylinder head sits on top of the cylinder and accommodates the spark plug. The shape of the cylinder head helps determine the volume of the combustion chamber. Because the cylinder head is subject to so much heat, it is also a major area that needs cooling. The piston is made of light alloy, with a single ring at the top that runs along the cylinder walls to seal in compression. The top of the piston, the cylinder head, and the cylinder barrel combine to create the combustion chamber.

The importance of oil mixed in with the fuel is for lubrication. As the fuel passes through the engine the oil lubricates the piston, connecting rod, crankshaft bearings, piston pin, and the cylinder walls.

The connecting rod is generally made from forged steel. It needs to be extremely strong to take the shock of the inertia at top dead center and at bottom dead center. A cage-style needle bearing is used at the top of the connecting rod to connect to the piston wrist pin and at the bottom of the rod to connect to the crankshaft.

The crankshaft is also made of steel and machined to fit bearings at each end. Most crankshafts are split style that

This is the piston rod and crankshaft layout of a two-stroke piston port engine. The orange color indicates the flow of hot exhaust gas from the combustion camber. *Jeff Deskins*

The HPV from Horstman Manufacturing of Vista, California, has been in service in the United States for a number of years. This engine can run in four classes, from junior to senior. *Jeff Deskins*

can be pulled apart to replace the bottom connecting rod bearing and the connecting rod. The center is offset to allow the crankshaft to rotate as the piston moves the connecting rod up and down.

It is the up and down motion created by all of these components that moves the air/fuel mixture through the engine and up into the combustion chamber.

The ignition of a two stroke delivers the spark that starts combustion. The initial electrical charge comes from a magneto that runs off the crankshaft. In most cases a two stroke does not require a battery to operate and can produce enough of its own electrical charge. The initial electrical pulse goes through an ignition box. The ignition box meters and coordinates the delivery of the pulse. From the ignition box, the charge goes to the coil, which amplifies the charge to the

voltage level required to jump the spark plug gap and ignite the air/fuel mixture.

Two-stroke engines can generate a great deal of heat, with the vast majority of it in the combustion chamber. Running a lean air/fuel mixture will cause intense heat at the point of combustion, when the piston is at TDC. The result is that the piston crown will actually begin to melt, which in turn will rob the engine of power and may lead to engine seizure. Also, when a two-stroke engine overheats, seizure of the piston skirt and the cylinder wall may occur. These two components literally weld together in an instant and stop the engine from turning. Another area susceptible to overheating is the combustion chamber itself.

The liquid cooling of engines has helped to increase the potential horsepower by keeping temperatures in an acceptable range as rpm levels rise. The added weight from a cooling system is more than made up for in increased power and longer engine life.

Yamaha KT100ES

The Yamaha KT100ES, or KT as it's commonly called, is by far the largest class of two-cycle karts in North America. This engine has been around for over 25 years and has had millions of hours of research and development. Some of the best racers in the world started with a KT. Some of the biggest classes you will find at local and national events are for the KT, and many sanctioning bodies run several different classes to accommodate different levels of age, weight, and skill.

The Yamaha KT100ES can run as a direct-drive or clutch kart. It can also run as a pipe or "can" kart. The term *can* refers to the type of exhaust pipe, which looks very much like a soup can. The first can was introduced as a three-hole version by RLV in 1986. The can setup was an attempt to create a user-friendly engine, since it eliminates much of the tuning requirements and complexities of running the open-pipe format. The can also reduces horsepower, which in turn reduces costs because the engine package and drive clutch are under less stress. The pipe setup makes use of a full expansion chamber, including a special section called the flex. This flex piece can be changed to tune the engine.

The KT is a great starting point for karters. It can be set up very simply and run very economically. Many drivers stay with the KT for years, making good use of the many things they learn along

The Yamaha KT100ES continues to be one of the most popular engines for sprint racing throughout the United States. It can run with different exhaust pipes to increase or reduce horsepower, depending on the class it's run in. *Sean Buur*

The ROTAX FR125 is one of the top electric-start two-stroke engines with many of the features, like the power valve, found on Ski-Doo and SeaDoo products. *Jeff Deskins*

The ROTAX engine uses a power valve mounted to the exhaust side of the cylinder to give the engine a little more horsepower by adjusting exhaust port timing as rpm increases. *Jeff Deskins*

the way. The pipe classes provide more speed and thrill, but require more tuning and attention than the can. Find the configuration that's right for you.

The KT is an air-cooled, piston port, two-cycle engine using a butterfly-style carburetor with low-speed and high-speed adjustments. The crankshaft drive is outward facing and uses a bearing support connected to the engine mount. The KT produces amazing power from a simple and compact design. There are no counterbalance shafts to reduce vibration. With the KT it doesn't get any simpler; this is what makes preparing and tuning the KT so critical—every little bit matters.

TAG Motor Package

The TAG rules package is truly the guideline to the next generation of two-cycle engines. This package combines many of the latest materials, designs, and performance features on a two-cycle motor to make it fast and reliable. The overall goal was to address the downsides of the two-cycle engines and still maintain the key benefits of high output with low weight. The engine was based on four main principles: environment, cost/maintenance, ease of use, and speed.

The first difference in these new generations of motors comes from the name itself. TAG actually is short for touch and go. The older generation of kart motors required an auxiliary starter. This also meant that you needed a second person to start you every time you wanted

to go onto the track—not an ideal situation, especially when you are trying to make karting easy and able to appeal to the recreational market. The TAG motors are equipped with an auxiliary battery with electric starter. This is a real advantage if you are at the track by yourself.

The next important consideration was to protect the environment from noise. Unlike the traditional air-cooled motors like the KT100, the TAG format calls for water-cooled motors. By water-cooling the engine, mechanical noise is reduced by approximately 40 percent compared to an air-cooled two-cycle engine. TAG drivers are also required to use CIK-approved intake silencers, and, by rules, are required to use the OEM exhaust silencer. The stock OEM silencers are designed to keep the noise to an acceptable decibel limit. Along with reducing noise, the intake silencer has a foam element filter to counteract the dirt-gathering effects of standard intake silencers and provide less engine wear.

The other area of concern was the high cost of competitive karting. By incorporating and designing an engine with bigger displacement than the traditional 100cc motor and by having a power band that works best with a lower rpm, rebuild and maintenance costs are greatly reduced. Expensive rebuild items, such as cylinders, are designed for long life with Gilnisil plating, shifting the rebuild costs to less-expensive components such as pistons and rings.

The technical specification manual supplied with most TAG motors is also quite good and very comprehensive. It covers everything from the spark plug to the exhaust pipe and all the parts in between. The recreational driver will only need to refer to specific parts of the manual, but eventually its best to be familiar with the entire book to insure that you won't run afoul in tech inspection, and that you're maximizing the performance of your engine.

TAG engines are required to use CIK approved intake silencers and OEM exhaust silencers.

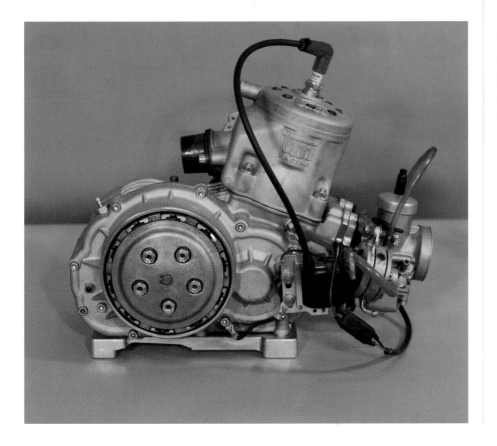

The TM Racing ICC engine uses a dry clutch. The plates in a dry clutch are not sealed in the crankcase and lubricated with oil, unlike moto engines. *Jeff Deskins*

The Honda CR 125 moto-style shifter kart engine is designed and built by Swedetech Racing of Elk Grove, California. This engine undergoes a significant transformation to go from a dirt bike to a kart. *Jeff Deskins*

SHIFTER 101

Overview

Shifter kart engines have transformed over the last few years. In North America, much of the early attention was focused on the moto-style engine, while in Europe much of the attention was on purpose-built engines called Intercontinental C or ICC. Over the last few years, the ICC engine has become more popular than the moto-style engine in North America. Each engine format has unique features and benefits. The moto engine is exactly as the name implies—these engines were designed and built for off-road motorcycles. Major motorcycle companies like Honda, Yamaha, Kawasaki, Suzuki, and TM build these engines.

Many modifications had to be developed to use these engines on a kart, including a special type of engine mount needed to accommodate a kart's mounting positions. The exhaust pipe also had to be modified. Because of the differences in power requirements and mounting limitations, the pipe for a bike is much different from what's required for a kart. Motocross bikes also use a wet clutch because they're designed to take the abuse of a riding technique that has the rider constantly slipping the clutch.

An ICC engine, on the other hand, is purpose-built to work only with karts. For that reason, the fit and finish look much nicer and less bulky on a kart than a moto engine. The major difference

Shifter motors use two

different types of clutches.

between the moto engine and the ICC engine is that the exhaust pipe exits to the rear and the intake is located on the front of the engine on an ICC. Almost without exception, at no other time will you slip the clutch, except at the start.

The transmission in a shifter motor is what really brings the package to life. It's a synchromesh design, which allows the gears to be selected in sequential order. There is a slight gap between first and second gear for neutral, a spot where no gear exists. This is an extremely compact transmission that allows for very rapid gear selection with minimal input. The only down side is that you must go through each gear. You cannot jump from fifth down to second in one movement.

Shifter motors use two different types of clutches. Whether a wet clutch or a dry clutch, they function the same way. The clutch is made of two types of interleaving plates called friction and drive plates. The main drive gear turns one set of plates, while the other set of plates drives the transmission gear. The plates are all gathered in a basket, one in between the other, pulled together by a set of springs. Friction forces the drive plates to turn the transmission plates. Pull the clutch lever and the plates move apart, taking the friction away, allowing the kart to run in gear while at a standstill. The wet clutch uses oil to keep the plates cool and widen the friction range. The release of a dry clutch is more like a switch, on or off.

ENGINE MAINTENANCE
Top-End Rebuild

Changing the piston and ring regularly is good engine maintenance. The cylinder, cylinder head, and possibly the connecting rod, will need attention at some point. This is where your engine builder can be your best source for coaching and advice on engine maintenance.

The CR125 engine from Swedetech Racing uses many specially-machined pieces to fit components like the ignition and fuel pump directly to the engine. *Jeff Deskins*

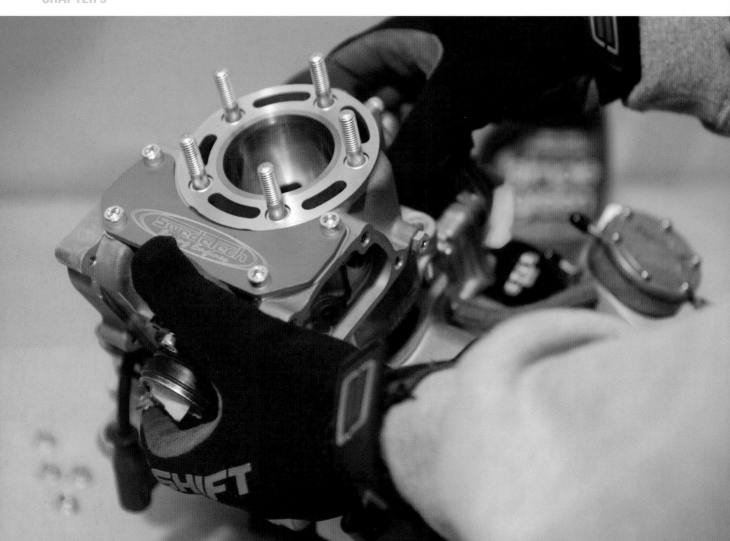

After the head has been removed, slowly pull the cylinder up using two hands to ensure that you do not scratch the cylinder. Remember that as the piston clears the cylinder wall, it will fall forward. Catch it from below. *Jeff Deskins*

Be sure to take the time to clean all parts before reassembly.

If you are rebuilding a water-cooled engine, you will need to drain the water first. Next remove the exhaust pipe completely. Remove the carburetor and the air breather. Pull off the plug cap and remove the spark plug; put the plug back in the box and check it later. Loosen the nuts on the head and at the base of the cylinder. Remove the head and place it on the bench with the top down, then lift the cylinder slowly from the crankcase. Make sure you have a clean rag to place the cylinder on, and place a clean rag around the connecting rod to protect the crankcase from any debris. Remove the old base gasket and the top gaskets from the cylinder and make sure the mounting surface is free of any debris.

Remove the old ring very carefully—make sure you do not scratch the piston. Remove one of the C-clips from the side of the piston; you can see a small indent that exposes part of the clip. Use a round, dull scribe to pop the clip out. Immediately throw the clip into the trash so you don't accidentally use it again. Push the pin out from the opposite side with your finger until it clears the bearing. Lift the piston off and push the pin all the way through. Remove the other C-clip and throw it into the trash along with the pin. If the piston is in good shape and measures to the proper tolerances, you may be able to reuse it in an emergency.

Be sure to take the time to clean all parts before reassembly. If you use a solvent tank, it's critical to wash your parts with warm soap and water as the final step before assembly. The cylinder should be cleaned and inspected before reassembly; check the cylinder walls for wear. Use PL50 and a green ScotchBrite pad to clean the cylinder bore. Clean in a cross pattern similar to the original pattern on the cylinder wall. Finally, wash the cylinder with soap and water and dry immediately. Inspect the head and clean as required. Polish it with an aluminum-polishing agent to finish.

Before rebuilding your engine, you must first determine which top end parts are worn. Proper measuring and comparing with the expected wear tolerances in your manual will tell you what to replace. Also, be sure to check with your engine builder.

As you assemble the top end, put a couple of drops of nonsynthetic two-cycle oil on each part before you put them together. Put the new ring on the new piston very carefully. Put a new C-clip into the piston and start the new pin into the piston on the opposite side. Place the piston over the rod, align the new bearing, and push the pin through very carefully. Once the pin is fully in place, put the other new C-clip into the piston.

With the piston and ring fitted you are ready to reassemble the engine. Start by coating the cylinder walls with a nonsynthetic two-cycle oil, then slide the cylinder back on. The base of the cylinder is slightly beveled. Squeeze the ring with one hand and slide the

Before rebuilding your engine, you must first determine which top end parts are worn.

As soon as the cylinder has been removed, place a clean rag around the crankcase opening so nothing falls into the bottom end of the engine. *Jeff Deskins*

Be very careful removing the old ring and placing the new one on the piston. Keep in mind that two-cycle pistons have a tiny notch located in the groove where the ring sits. The notch in the ring must match up to this. *Jeff Deskins*

If your engine is brand new or has a new top end, you need to do a basic engine break-in.

cylinder on. Once in place, put the nuts on so they are finger tight.

Tighten the bolts on the cylinder in a cross pattern starting with the right front. Put on the head and tighten a little at a time in a cross pattern as well. Refer to the owner's manual or check with your engine builder for the correct torque settings.

Basic Engine Break-In

If your engine is brand new or has a new top end, you need to do a basic engine break-in. Ask your engine builder what the proper jetting is for engine break-in. With the engine fired, place your hand on the cylinder and feel the engine come up to temperature. This should take between five and ten minutes. While the engine is running, always vary the rpm at the low end of the rpm

range. Shut the engine down and allow it to cool. Check for leaks around the head, valve cover, carburetor, and header pipe.

With the engine cooled down, strap on your gear and head out on the track. Gently roll into the throttle as you exit the corners and roll out of the throttle before you get the rpm too high. Prolonged high rpm will damage an engine on break-in. It is important that you vary your rpm on the track in order to seat the ring properly. This session should last about 10 minutes. With a four-stroke engine, when you come off the track, drain the oil from the crankcase after the engine has cooled—never remove the drain plug on a hot engine. Check the drained oil for contaminants, then refill the crankcase with new oil.

For a brand-new engine or a complete rebuild, it's usually a good idea to do three 10-minute sessions, adding higher rpm with each session. After break-in is complete, change the jetting to the proper settings indicated by your engine builder and put in a fresh plug.

Engine Storage

If your engine is to be stored for 60 days or more, some preventive measures must be taken to avoid deterioration. After cleaning off all the grease, grit, and grime, you need to prepare the engine [for] long-term storage. First, drain the [fuel] tank, fuel lines, and the carburetor [float] bowl, just as after each race day. [Take] the carburetor off and spray it with [carb]uretor cleaner. Move the slide up [and] down, making sure the carburetor [is fr]ee of any fuel. Put the carburetor [bac]k on and place a rag in the end.

[ ] Remove the entire exhaust system. [Wi]pe the pipe and silencer down [tho]roughly and apply a generous [co]ating of WD-40 to keep any surfaces [fro]m rusting. Place in a large plastic bag [an]d place in your seat. Put a clean rag in [th]e exhaust port. Next, remove the [sp]ark plug and spray a little WD-40 [in]to the combustion chamber. With the [p]lug in the plug cap and properly [g]rounded, put the kart in gear and turn [th]e rear wheels. This will coat the [c]ylinder walls with a protective coating. [P]ut the spark plug back in.

Next you need to think about draining the water out of the cooling

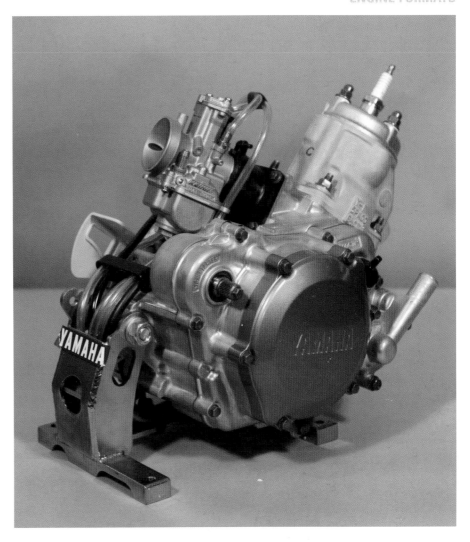

system. This is only necessary if the temperature in your area will fall below freezing, otherwise leave the water in and top it off as required. To drain the system, start by loosening the hose clamp at the water pump. For moto engines this is at the front of the engine. Loosen the radiator cap and tilt the kart to the right. For ICC-style engines, the pump is at the back of the kart. Tilt the kart backward to make sure all the water runs out.

The Yamaha YZ 85 is used in junior shifter kart racing classes. This engine can be run as a novice shifter package by using a restrictor plate on the intake and exhaust.
Jeff Deskins

Chapter 4

KARTING SAFETY

The start of any race is exciting and action packed. Here racers take to the track during the Quincy in the Park Race held each year in Quincy, Illinois. *Sean Buur*

Invest in safety before you invest in your kart.

WHY IS SAFETY SO IMPORTANT?

Kart racing is a fast-paced high-speed sport where competitors test their skills and those of the other drivers in very close quarters. It's critical that safety always be a prime consideration to keep all competitors, spectators, and race officials safe from injury. While you can never completely eliminate injury in any sport, you can certainly take many steps to greatly reduce the possibility of serious harm.

All motor-racing organizations, including your local kart club, require specific safety equipment that must meet stringent international standards. Do not take the importance of safety equipment lightly. Too many drivers will spend excessive amounts of money on their engines and then buy the cheapest helmet they can find. O[ur?] good friend Ross Bentley, author of t[he] *Speed Secrets* car racing book ser[ies] says: "If you can't afford a good helme[t] you *can't* afford to race."

So be sure to invest in safety befo[re] you invest in your kart.

Today's race karts have numerou[s] safety features. Over the years, ka[rt] manufacturers and racing organization[s] have worked together to develop bumper, nerf-bar, and bodywork systems to keep drivers safe. Bumpers help protect the feet, while nerf bars keep wheels from becoming tangled. Today's kart bodywork has also been tested for impact absorption. In case of collision, injuries may result if a kart flips over. Impact-absorbing bodywork helps keep karts from flipping. Though such incidents are rare, and race programs typically run the whole day without incident, as a new karter, it's nice to know that safety has been so well thought out by kart manufacturers.

Respect for your fellow competitors and your track officials is vital to enjoying a fun day at the track. One of the best safety tools you can bring to the track is a positive attitude. Make sure you are karting to have fun and enjoy a day of competition. Remember, most clubs are run by volunteers who spend their own time to ensure that you have a fun, safe day at the track.

TRACK SAFETY

All kart tracks are designed to meet basic safety standards set forth by the karting industry and international motorsports groups like the CIK/FIA. This includes the use of barriers and fences to keep both racers and spectators safe. Outdoor tracks are designed to have a lot of runoff area between the

One of the best safety tools you can bring to the track is a positive attitude.

Kart drivers must have all their safety gear on and be ready to race when on grid. Race readiness is something you don't want to rush. *Sean Buur*

ur
he
ies
et,
...ficials, like Paul Zalud of
S...re... f Karting, are a key source of
inf...on during a race weekend.
Mo...s... organizations have a
centr...rd for information posting.
Jeff D...s

racing surface and the barriers. Indoor tracks use specific barriers made of plastic that are designed to keep karts from crossing into other parts of the track. Indoor and outdoor barriers are also designed to absorb impacts to help keep drivers safe.

Track safety includes the use of signal flags, driver hand signals, and pit area safety. A key component of safety is good communication and awareness of your environment.

SIGNAL FLAGS
If you've spent any time watching motorsports, you're probably familiar with the basic racing flags.

Track safety includes the use of signal flags, driver hand signals, and pit area safety. A key component of safety is good communication and awareness of your environment.

Racing flags are not much different from the many road signs and stoplights we encounter on streets and highways every day. Just as we need to obey those signals in traffic, we need

to understand and obey all the flags on the track. Ignoring flags is not an option and can lead to serious injury if you choose to not pay attention. Always check with your local club and sanctioning body to confirm the types of flags and their use in your area.

Green

The *green* flag is for go. This flag is displayed at the start of the race and sometimes after the first lap to signal to the drivers that they are racing. Racing does not begin until this flag is displayed. Be sure not to accelerate before you are shown the green flag as this can cause an accident.

Yellow

The *yellow* flag means caution, trouble ahead on the track. If the corner worker is waving the yellow, it means that there is an incident in that corner. If the workers

are holding the yellow still but open, it means that the incident is further down the track. Either way, you need to be aware of trouble ahead, which may require you to change your line and slow down. Once clear of the trouble or when the yellow has been dropped by the workers, you can resume racing. Some tracks also use a full-course yellow. Usually this is shown by each corner marshal holding two yellow flags. In this case, the leader is meant to slow down gradually, until the field is packed up. Once the field is lined up in single-file order and the incident is cleared, the race will be restarted at the start/finish line. Whether the yellow flag is local or full course you cannot pass under the yellow flag. Passing will result in a penalty.

Sometimes at the start of a race you may see a corner marshal wave the yellow flag in a downward motion as a signal to slow down for the start. After a

Race flags you will encounter during your race day include green, yellow, red, blue, black, and checkered.
Craig Ketchen

Whether the yellow flag is local or full course, you cannot pass under the yellow flag. Passing will result in a penalty.

When a major incident occurs, race officials are on the scene quickly to display the proper flag. *Sean Buur*

If you receive a black flag, go into the pits immediately.

THE MEATBALL FLAG

The meatball flag means that something's wrong with your kart. It gets the name "meatball" from the big red dot in the middle of a black background. This flag is usually shown because something fell off of your kart, quite possibly due to contact. Even though you can't see it or hear it, you may have a serious mechanical problem with your kart that requires immediate attention. Your kart could be leaking water or a bumper could be falling off. It's important that you immediately reduce speed, check for traffic, get off the racing line, and exit the track at the pit entrance. Tracks without a meatball flag will use the black flag.

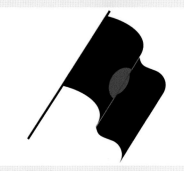

Craig Ketchen

race is over, many tracks wave the yellow flags around the track to signal that the race is over and the field is frozen. Again, do not pass under these yellow-flag conditions.

Red

The *red* flag means *stop*. If a red flag appears on the track at any point, raise your hand and pull to the edge of the track and *stop*. It is critical to not slam on the brakes and cause a pile up of karts behind you. After stopping, turn off your engine and stay by your kart. *Do not* remove your helmet. Wait for the race officials to give you instructions.

During a red flag there may be safety vehicles or race officials on the racing surface. Never start your kart until the all-clear has been given from the race officials. Once restarted, follow the race officials' instructions. Most clubs restart the drivers in their position from the last completed lap.

Black

The *black* flag usually means you may have done something wrong on the track. If you receive a black flag, go into the pits immediately. You'll probably have a discussion with a race official about improper behavior or rough driving on the track.

In some cases, a race director may give you a rolled black, which is a warning that you need to stop the rough driving and clean up your act. Do it again and you'll get the full black.

This is the flag every drivers looks forward to seeing at the end of a hard fought race . . . *Sean Buur*

After stopping, turn off your engine and stay by your kart. Do not remove your helmet.

If you are shown the blue flag make no sudden or quick movements.

... and the driver who sees it first will get a chance to show off the victory in style. *Sean Buur*

Some racing series will display a sign-board with the driver's number along with the black flag. This makes it easier to signal the driver when karts are running close together.

It is not wise to ignore the black flag. This only hurts you and your fellow competitors, and could cause you to lose your racing privileges. It also shows a lack of respect for the officials. Keep in mind that black flags are not always for driving infractions. On many occasions the black flag is used to signal a kart driver that he may have a mechanical problem or safety issue.

Blue

The *blue* flag means you're being lapped. You need to yield the racing line to the leaders coming through.

Many new drivers seem to struggle with this flag because they try so hard to get out of the way, they actually create an incident on the racetrack. If you are shown the blue flag, the important thing to remember is to make no sudden or quick movements. First, try to figure out how close the passing karts are to you. When they are close, yield the racing line by pointing the leaders by on the side you want them to pass on. Then, at the same time, slowly ease off the throttle. Wait until the faster karts have passed before you rejoin going at your race pace. It's important that you learn to work with other drivers under this blue flag condition. Some day, you will be passing lap traffic and will appreciate the help.

Checkered

The *checkered* flag signals the end of the race. Everyone wants to be the first across the finish line and see the checkered flag. After you cross the line and receive the checkered flag the course goes under caution. Stay in order, do not pass, and proceed to the pit entrance.

DRIVER SIGNALS

Karts do not come equipped with brake lights or turn signals, so driver hand signals become very important to keep karts from colliding. The most important hand signal is raising your hand up for braking or slowing. This is used any time that you are not up to speed on the track. This may include your first lap while you get your tires up to temperature or when you are approaching an on-track incident. Your raised hand lets drivers behind you know that you are slowing or stopping and they'll have time to take evasive action to avoid a collision. You will see drivers use this hand signal as they enter or exit the track. In the case of a red flag, when a driver has to stop very quickly, they may actually wave their arm.

Always look before you enter the track from the pit lane. Many kart tracks will have a grid marshal who controls the entry of karts onto the racing surface. When there is no grid marshal, enter with caution and raise your hand. Keep off the racing line if possible and

Memo Gidley points a driver past during his annual karting clinic in Hawaii. Kart drivers use hand signals to communicate to other drivers while on the track. *Earl Ma*

The most important hand signal is raising your hand up for braking or slowing.

A helmet must fit snug, yet be comfortable. There should be no gap between the padding and your cheeks. *Sean Buur*

Always use great care and keep a properly rated fire extinguisher at the ready.

get up to speed quickly. Be aware of oncoming traffic.

When exiting the racing surface, be sure to give karts behind you lots of advanced warning. Don't suddenly peel off into the pits. Raise your hand as you approach the pit entrance and begin to slow down. Before exiting, always test your brakes by pushing on them gently.

PIT SAFETY

Also important to a fun, safe day of racing is proper pit safety. It's your responsibility to keep your pit area clean and safe. Be sure to use power tools with care and remember that race engines can be very hot. Be sure to have an adequate first-aid kit handy for small

cuts and burns. For major cuts and burns, go see the on-site emergency medical technicians (EMT).

Kart racing involves the use of gasoline, flammable lubricants, cleaners, and many different oils. Always be careful when handling fuel of any kind. Try to keep all your fuel containers in a shaded and vented area. Keep them out of reach of small children. Always use great care and keep a properly rated fire extinguisher at the ready.

SAFETY HELMETS

A helmet is the most important item in your kart racing kit. Your helmet must fit well, meet current safety standards, and be kept clean. Keep in

mind that a helmet for kart racing is different than a helmet for car racing. Both are made to the same design and manufacturing standards for safety, but a car racing helmet must be fire resistant. For these helmets the inside liner is made of Nomex, a fire-resistant material. A car-racing helmet can be used for karting, but a karting helmet cannot be used for car racing. Kart helmets are rated M, the same as motorcycle helmets.

A racing helmet has four different components: a rigid outer shell, a

Many drivers have their helmets painted. Here is a Bell GTX helmet painted for Secrets of Speed by Mike Corby of Corby Concepts in Indianapolis, Indiana. Be sure to have your helmet painted by a experienced helmet painter to ensure that there is no damage to the shell or lining of the helmet. *Sean Buur*

crushable liner, a chin strap, and comfort padding. The rigid outer shell adds load-spreading capacity and prevents objects from penetrating the helmet. The liner absorbs the energy of an impact by crushing. The chin strap, when properly buckled and adjusted, along with the padding, helps the helmet remain in position during a crash.

The shield is another area of importance. Generally made of Lexan, a bulletproof material, the shield provides a clear field of vision and protects the eyes from flying debris such as rocks. Take good care of your shield, because scratches will impair your vision. Different shield finishes are not just for looks, but serve a purpose to block bright sunlight or enhance the landscape in low-light situations.

What helps drivers and race organizers stay on top of driver safety is the Snell Foundation's helmet safety rating system. The protective capability of a particular helmet is difficult to measure. The Snell Foundation tests and destroys thousands of helmets every year to determine how safe they are. Snell certification is an assurance that a helmet has measured up to the highest standards for protective performance.

Drivers need to understand that helmets don't last forever. Just because it still fits and looks good doesn't mean that you're getting the best protection. We recommend that you replace your helmet at least every five years. Glues, resins, and other materials used in helmet production can affect liner materials, and normal wear and tear contribute to helmet degradation.

Taking good care of your helmet is also key to its durability. Storing it in a protective bag and carefully packing it is very helpful. Be careful not to drop your helmet on the ground; many manufacturers recommend that if you drop your helmet on the ground you should replace it. Other factors, like ultraviolet rays, can break down the helmet from the outside. Additionally, there will be a noticeable improvement in the protective characteristic of helmets over a five-year period due to advances in materials, design, and standards. Consult your manufacturers' website for up-to-date information on your make and model.

If your helmet is Snell approved, it will have a sticker inside. The adhesive label or decal is usually affixed to the inside of the helmet. If it isn't visible, check underneath the flaps of the comfort padding. Having this label in your helmet is a pre-race safety tech item that is checked at the track. Without it, you won't be allowed to race.

Your race helmet needs to be snug. It should not be so tight that it hurts or so loose that it flops around. Due to varying shapes, heads that are apparently the same size when measured by a tape may not necessarily fit the same size helmet. Always check your helmet fit with a trained professional. Several steps will help you find a helmet that fits well.

Measuring your head accurately is the first step to correct helmet fit. A cloth tape should be used to make the initial measurement. The circumference of the head should be measured at a point approximately 1 inch above the eyebrows in front, and at a point in the back of the head that results in the largest possible measurement. Take several measurements to make sure you have the largest one.

Once the helmet model and size have been selected, try it on before you buy it. Grasp the helmet by the chin straps and place your thumbs inside the surface of the straps. Spread the fitting foam apart and slip the helmet over your head. Check for helmet movement; see if the helmet moves from side to side or up and down. It needs to be snug, and your cheeks should be firm in the cheek padding. Fasten the chin strap and try to pull the helmet off. There should be no excess pressure at any point. A helmet is like a pair of shoes—it will break in a bit but not a lot.

SAFETY GEAR

The rest of your safety gear is made up of several items. These include a race suit, gloves, race shoes, a neck collar, and a chest or rib protector. Each of these items is equally important to ensuring maximum safety while racing. Like your helmet, safety gear is not an area you want to skimp on. Good-quality equipment that is well cared for can be resold very easily. Be sure that all of your safety equipment fits properly— not too small, and not too big. This is especially important for children, where we tend to want to get that next season out of our children's equipment.

Race Suits

Your race suit is what comes between you and the track surface in the case of an accident. It needs to meet certain abrasion and skid resistance requirements. Kart race suits don't need to be fireproof. In fact, manufacturers can't use Nomex in a kart suit because it has no abrasion resistance. Your suit needs to fit comfortably; make sure you have ample room in the arms and shoulders to give you full range of motion. Look for extra leg length so the bottom cuff doesn't ride up and expose your lower leg while seated. Most good race suits

For a detailed fitting guide go to the Bell Racing Helmets website at www.bellracing.com.

If your helmet is Snell approved, it will have a sticker inside.

Memo Gidley in his full karting gear, including shoes, suit, gloves, helmet support, and helmet. Be sure your suit is in good condition and fits you properly. A clean suit will last longer and fit better over time. *Sean Buur*

SAFETY GEAR
CHEST PROTECTORS

For junior racers in the United States, it will be mandatory to have a chest protector starting in the 2006 racing season. Chest protectors specifically target the chest or sternum area of the driver. For children under the age of 13, this area is especially vulnerable in certain types of crashes, such as a direct front-end collision. The result of the impact could be a soft tissue or bruising of the vital organs found within the chest cavity area. While these injuries are extremely rare, don't take a chance when there are great products available.

There are SFI certified and approved chest protectors that are complete units, which cover ribs and chest, or units that will work in conjunction with a rib protector. The important distinct with these new breed of chest protectors is that there is no gap, zipper, or Velcro at the chest/sternum area. These vests connect on the sides and provide a solid uninterrupted protection of the front area.

Two companies leading the way in junior driver safety protection are Armadillo (aargear.com) and Ribtec. Both have been SFI certified and provide great products. More companies will be offering similar units in the coming years. Be sure to check with your local club or racing organization for complete details. Bottom-line, even if you can race without one, why would you. Invest in safety, it could last a lifetime.

It's a great idea for junior drivers to wear a chest protector. This unit made by Armadillo helps protect the chest area against impact from the steering wheel.

---

have vents for cooling and stretch panels for comfort.

Keep your suit clean. Leaving your suit bunched up in your gear bag will shorten its life and make it look bad. Always hang your suit up in the garage to air it out after a day at the track. Follow the basic care instructions provided by the manufacturer. Don't be afraid to wash your suit; leaving grease and grime on your suit is far more damaging than any rinse cycle.

Gloves

Gloves need to fit well to give you a good feel for the steering wheel. Wearing gloves with good flexibility and good traction on your steering wheel will keep your forearms from tiring as quickly. Try to keep your gloves clean inside and out. To work on your kart, mechanic's gloves help keep your hands clean and free from grease. Make sure you wash your hands before you put your race gloves on—getting them greasy inside or out reduces the grip on the wheel and ruins the suede on the steering wheel as well.

Race Shoes

Race shoes are important because they give you a good feel for the pedals. They come in low-cut and high-top versions. The thin, smooth sole lets you feel the brake and gas pedals. Good flexibility, which helps with smooth throttle and brake application, is also important. Make sure they have good heel padding and protection. Good race shoes will have a Velcro strap at the top to hold the laces in place, making sure they don't get caught on anything.

Neck Support

A neck support or neck collar is a critical safety item and is mandatory in all North American races, and in most races around the world. It protects the collarbone from impact from the edges

Wearing gloves with good flexibility and good traction on your steering wheel will keep your forearms from tiring as quickly.

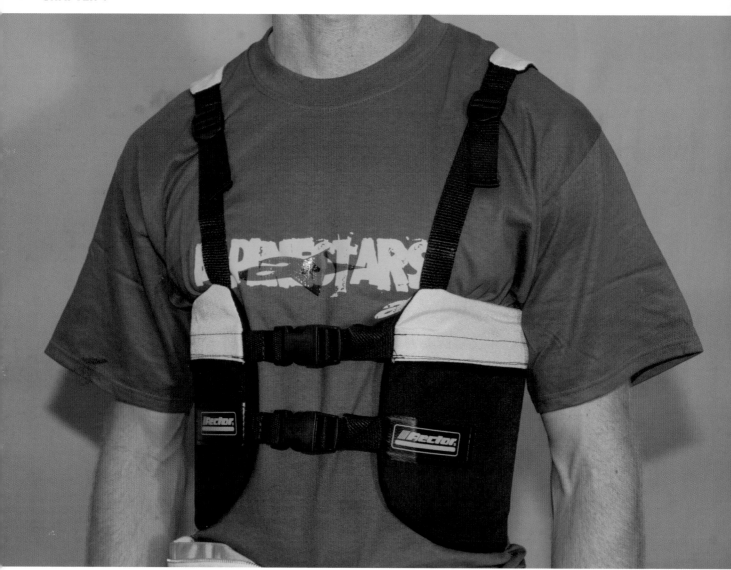

A good rib protector is made of hard plastic wrapped in durable foam and covered in a strong nylon material. The vest needs to be very adjustable to ensure maximum comfort. There are styles made for both men and women. *Jeff Deskins*

Upper body protection is a critical part of driver safety.

of the helmet. Also, it protects the neck from hyperextension and possible fracture. Many neck collars are made with double Velcro fasteners to ensure that the neck support stays in place. Not only is it unsafe to have a neck collar fall off while driving, it's also a way to get black flagged during a race. Some neck collars have removable foam padding that can be adjusted for your neck length. It's important to have enough foam to make it safe but not so much that you lose a lot of range of motion.

Rib Protectors

Upper body protection is a critical part of driver safety. There are both rib protectors

and chest protectors; the important point is that not all rib protectors are chest protectors. Rib protectors are not mandatory everywhere but are certainly a great idea. In the event of a serious side impact, they protect your ribs from injury. The side of the kart seat is not well padded, and the rib protector offers a layer of comfort and protection. For Junior racers—kids under the age of 13—it's important to have a vest with built-in sternum protection in case you hit the steering wheel with your chest. It's personal preference if you wear your rib protector under or over your driving suit. The benefit to wearing it underneath is that it has less chance of getting caught on anything.

KART SAFETY

The first major step in kart safety is a complete nut-and-bolt check. Put a wrench on every nut and bolt, checking for solid contact on the washers. Replace worn, bent, or stripped bolts immediately. Many bolts on a kart need to be cotter pinned, C-clipped, or safety wired. Cotter-pinned bolts require a hole at the end for the cotter pin to fit through. Bolts that are wired require the end of one bolt to be wired to the end of another. An example of this is the bolts that hold the brake rotor to the brake-rotor hub. Always safety wire in the direction that holds the bolt tight. Some karts have bolts with the ends machined to accommodate a C-clip.

Starting at the front with the steering system, check all of the hardware such as the spindle bolts, inner and outer tie-rod jam nuts, and the bolts holding the steering column at the bottom and at the steering post. All of the steering-system bolts need to be cotter pinned or C-clipped. All of these connections are safety items that are required to pass technical inspection before competition.

The next area that needs extra attention is the brake system. Make sure the pivot bolt on the brake pedal is pinned and the pedal is free to move without binding. The connecting rod must have safety clips at each end. You can use a small tye wrap around the safety clip for added security. We recommend that you attach a piece of braided wire from the brake pedal to the rear-brake master cylinder as a safety backup. Make sure that the safety cable has enough slack to allow the pedal to move freely.

For safety, the bolts holding the master cylinder in place need to be safety wired or cotter pinned. The bolts

Check your brake system regularly for any leaking or cracks. Be sure that all of your brake lines are in good shape and free from any chaffing or sharp bends and all of the bolts are safety wired. *Sean Buur*

All of the steering-system bolts need to be cotter pinned or C-clipped.

Replace worn, bent, or stripped bolts immediately.

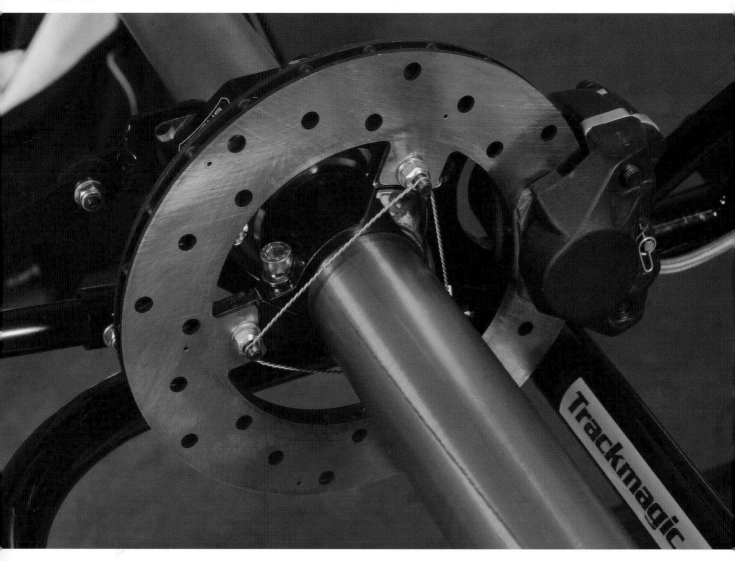

The rear brake rotor is wired to ensure it does not fall off. In some cases, a self-locking nut will also be used. *Sean Buur*

that hold the brake calipers to the mounting brackets will also need to be wired together. Whenever you are wiring bolts such as caliper bolts, for safety, it is critical that the wire is attached in a way so that it pulls in the direction that the bolt tightens. This will help to ensure that the bolts don't loosen. We also recommend that you use stainless-steel wire and the appropriate wire pliers. It takes a little practice to wire correctly, so be patient.

Look over the brake lines and make sure they flow smoothly and are secured to the frame with the proper clips or tye wraps. The goal is to hold the lines firmly in place without pinching them. The brake pedal connecting rod and

the left tie rod should not interfere with each other when the steering wheel is turned from side to side. Check the brake fluid level and top it off, if necessary. Be careful—if spilled, brake fluid will remove paint and tarnish most finished surfaces.

Next, check the throttle or gas pedal, making sure the pivot bolt is cotter pinned and the pedal moves freely. We recommend that the gas pedal have two springs to ensure that the gas pedal will return even if one spring breaks. The throttle cable should flow smoothly up to the carburetor. If the cable has any kinks, replace it immediately. Make sure the outer casing doesn't touch the engine, which may melt the housing, causing the pedal to stick. For smooth gas pedal operation, use a cable casing with a nylon inner housing.

The next area to check is around the rear axle and bearing cassette mounting supports, making sure the bolts are tight and secure. Make sure the axle is set to an even distance on both sides and set the hubs at an equal distance from the end of the axle. Axle collars or setscrews used to hold the axle in the bearings should be checked for tightness. Use blue Loctite to keep setscrews in place or they will work loose very quickly.

The final areas to check are the front and rear bumpers, bodywork, and floorpan. Most karts run standard CIK side pods and nose cone. Nerf bars are one of the most critical safety elements and should be visually inspected for cracks or signs of wear. All of these components need to be secured using Nylock nuts. Look for connections that are isolated with rubber washers. Most of these connections need only be snug. A kart has both a front and rear bumper. For safety reasons, most karts are designed to have tight front bumper bolts.

All of the front-end components, such as the king pin pictured here, need to be clipped or pinned to ensure nuts do not fall off the bolts. *Sean Buur*

Chapter 5

KART SETUP

Karts are designed to lift the inside rear wheel, allowing the kart to turn a corner without scrubbing the tires.
Todd McCall

The flex of the chassis and its components help turning, while the rubber from the tires creates grip.

The basic design of any kart chassis uses a solid axle, or live axle as it is sometimes called, which locks the rear wheels together by way of a single axle. By contrast, a race car uses a differential in the rear end that allows the inside wheel to rotate less than the outside wheel. A differential is used to help a race car turn through a corner by allowing the drive wheels to rotate independently as they travel through a different radius. A kart relies on weight jacking and the flex of the chassis, allowing the inside rear wheel to lift off the ground, to help the kart turn through a corner.

For setup, everything we do to our kart is based on lifting the inside rear wheel for the right amount of time. If we can't lift the inside rear wheel, or at least remove most of the weight from that

tire, the kart simply will not turn. The front and rear of the kart must share the available grip. This is called balance. The flex of the chassis and its components help turning, while the rubber from the tires creates grip. When tuning your kart, you need to find that right amount of flex to balance that grip and allow the kart to turn efficiently.

In this section, we will cover a lot of the areas that contribute to kart performance. These include chassis design, the seat, data acquisition, driveline, tires, and proper maintenance. Carefully addressing each of these areas will ensure that your kart is race ready.

HOW A KART CHASSIS WORKS
In every type of karting, the setup of each component is critical, as each component plays a role in the handling

and tuning of the kart chassis. The main force that is active in helping to steer your kart is weight transfer. This transfer of weight from one tire to another is by design and will influence the handling of a kart in many different ways. Other factors to be considered include track width, center of gravity, and track conditions.

The role of the front end is to control the direction and stability of the kart at speed. The geometry built into the frame and spindles causes a weight-jacking effect, which helps the inside rear wheel to lift. The most important element of the front-end design is commonly referred to as king pin inclination (KPI) and is designed by the chassis manufacturer based on the

engine type and its intended use. KPI not only causes the inside front wheel to drop and the outside front wheel to rise in relation to each other, but it also affects the attitude of the tire to the track surface. KPI is made up of caster and camber, two different angles that work together to help a kart change direction quickly and efficiently.

The first and most important angle is the caster angle, or the rearward angle, that the front spindle has in relation to vertical or plumb. A kart will never have zero caster (vertical) or negative caster (forward lean), as this will not allow weight jacking to occur. All karts have positive caster built into them through the positioning of the spindle yoke welded to the chassis. As more

The king pin angles inward at the top and forward at the bottom. The result is a change in height and attitude of the tire as the wheel is turned, causing a shift in weight on each tire.
Sean Buur

The role of the front end is to control the direction and stability of the kart at speed.

The front spindle is long, allowing inward or outward front tire movement using spacers, which is used to help improve kart handling.
Sean Buur

Toe angle is the relationship of the front tires to each other.

caster angle is applied, more weight jacking will occur on the kart.

The second angle is the camber angle or the inward angle that the kingpin has in relation to plumb. All karts have some camber built into the spindle yoke. However, much of this angle is removed in the design of the spindle stub axle, leaving zero camber on most karts. Camber angle changes will affect the attitude of the tires to the track surface during cornering and straightline driving, along with affecting the weight jacking characteristics.

Both camber and caster can be added or removed using special "pills" or bushings, which are set into the top of the yoke where the spindle bolt goes

through. The pill has an offset hole, usually at specific degrees from center. As the pill is rotated to the outside, caster is removed and positive camber is added. As the pill is turned inward, again the caster is removed and this time negative camber is added. These pills can be rotated a full 360 degrees, having varying effects on the chassis.

Toe angle is the relationship of the front tires to each other. Zero-toe means that the wheels are parallel to each other. Toe-in, or negative toe, means that the tires point in toward each other. Toe-out, or positive toe, means that the tires point away from each other.

Ackerman has an effect on the front wheels as the steering is turned. It uses the angle of the spindle arms and offset holes on the steering shaft to make the inner wheel turns in more than the outer wheel. This causes the inside front wheel to turn on a tighter radius than the outside front wheel, reducing tire scrub and helping with grip while cornering. Along with this, adding Ackerman will also increase the weight-jacking effect, and help weight transfer.

The role of the rear of the kart is to deliver power and accelerate the kart forward. Axles, bearings, and hubs work together to control axle flex and maintain traction through a corner. There are a number of different axle lengths, diameters, and thicknesses to choose from that can be combined with a number of different hub lengths. The end result is the same: controlling the flex of the axle to provide the perfect amount of inside wheel lift and compliancy.

Just like the suspension on a street car helps absorb bumps and create a stable ride, a kart's axle will create a stable, fast kart. The goal on a race-track is to get the kart turned and get the rear wheels planted back on the track as soon as possible. The quicker the horsepower can be delivered to the ground with both wheels, the better the acceleration and the faster you will go.

The most critical area on the back of the kart is where the axle is located. The axle is mounted on bearings, which sit inside bearing cassettes. The

The role of the rear of the kart is to deliver power and accelerate the kart forward.

The rear axle needs to spin and flex at the same time. The unique shape of the bearing and bearing cassettes help this happen easily. *Sean Buur*

Kart seats are not placed in the center, but to the left side of the kart. This offsets the weight of the engine.
Sean Buur

The seat can control the weight transfer, center of gravity, chassis flex, and weight balance.

role of the bearing cassette is to hold the bearing firmly, yet allow the frame rails to move and twist with minimal friction and allow the axle to rotate freely and let the chassis flex. These cassettes are bolted to hangers. The bearing cassette hanger can adjust the ride height and wheelbase by providing different alignment holes or positioning bushings.

The role of the chassis is to join the input from the front end and the back end of the kart. When properly adjusted, it should provide just the right amount of flex or resistance to achieve optimum turning and bump-absorbing performance. A number of components can be clamped onto or removed from a

chassis to help manage this flex. The purpose of these bars is to stiffen or soften the chassis.

SEAT DYNAMICS 101

The seat is one of the most critical components of a kart because it's the seat that connects the largest mass—the driver—to the kart. Too often the seat is improperly positioned or poorly installed, directly affecting the handling performance of the chassis. The seat can control the weight transfer, center of gravity, chassis flex, and weight balance. A properly installed seat will complement these forces, while a poorly installed seat will work against the chassis, causing a number of handling problems. A well-installed, properly fitted seat can mean seconds in a lap.

Like the geometry and flex built into the chassis, kart manufacturers spend a lot of time on seat positioning. Most manufacturers have recommended settings for optimum performance; these are available from your dealer or from the manufacturer's website. You should always consult your chassis manufacturer or your seat manufacturer for exact mounting specifications.

When installing your seat, take into consideration driver size, track conditions, tire type, and engine style. The position of the seat can be adjusted to ensure maximum performance from each of these elements. Drivers must learn that, like tires, the seat is a commodity that gets consumed. Top drivers will change seats regularly to maintain consistent handling performance. This is especially relevant to North American drivers who may run street races during which the seat can hit the ground, sustaining significant damage.

The seat affects the transfer of weight, the flex of the chassis, the weight balance of the kart, and the center of gravity. All of these help to pick up and set down the inside rear wheel, which is required to help the kart handle properly through a corner. As the geometry of the chassis transfers weight, the seat affects this by transferring more or less of the driver's mass. The force applied by the driver as the kart changes direction enhances this weight transfer as the driver's body pushes outward on the seat when the kart turns through a corner. The seat can control how much of this energy is transferred. A loose or incorrectly fitted seat can create an unnecessary transfer of weight and throw off the balance of the kart. The

weight of the driver can slosh if the seat isn't bolted in properly or if the seat is too big for the driver.

DATA ACQUISITION

Data acquisition is the collection of real-time information and the process of analyzing that information to determine if modifications have made you faster or slower. Each time you modify the setup of your kart, you hope for a positive result. Data acquisition allows you to determine if a particular tweak helped or hurt the overall performance of your kart. Data acquisition is a gauge of your progress throughout the day. The most critical and difficult part of data acquisition is finding *relevant* information in the data you've acquired.

Data-acquisition systems are not a magic genie that tells you how to go faster. You need to be very careful not to let data acquisition steer you in the

Some kart seats come with no padding while others are partially or fully padded. It's really the driver's choice for comfort. *Sean Buur*

A well-installed, properly fitted seat can mean seconds in a lap.

The data acquisition unit displays important information like rpm, lap time, and engine temperature. This is the Mychron Plus system from Aimsports, which uses lights, a backlit display, and numbers to indicate the important information to the driver. *Sean Buur*

Some data acquisition companies have steering wheels that hold the data unit inside. While most data units can fit on any steering wheel, these make for a nice clean fit. *Sean Buur*

Data acquisition will help you gain that extra tenth of a second.

wrong direction by misreading the numbers. In fact, racers who simply look at the minimum and maximum values per lap often make a common critical error, basing crucial adjustments on this vague data. The ability to see where the data is happening instead of simply when it happened makes all the difference.

Although not cheap, a data-acquisition system is a good investment. When used properly, data acquisition will help

you gain that extra tenth of a second. Regardless of what system you buy, always consult the manufacturer for correct mounting, use, and care. The manufacturer is your best source of information to ensure that you get the most from your data-acquisition unit.

The first goal is to understand all of the key readings that data acquisition can draw on; they will help you understand what you're measuring. The power of data acquisition is the ability to make changes to your kart based on very specific information, which will back up your seat-of-the-pants feeling.

Capturing Relevant Real-Time Data

A data-acquisition system is actually quite simple to install. You don't need a degree in engineering or computer science to make it work. However, it does take time to learn your specific system and understand how it will work best for you.

In many basic applications, the display dash and brain box are housed in a single unit. This main unit connects all of the sensor leads to the processor and memory. It also sends information to the dash for real-time presentation, or to a laptop for analysis by special software. The main unit carries the hardware and software that brings the input data to life. This can be a separate unit or can be integrated into the display dash.

The main unit with the display dash attaches to the steering wheel to give the driver real-time heads-up information on what the sensors are reading. Most systems use numbers and lights to indicate the current status of engine

output parameters as well as on-track performance. The main display feature is usually engine operating temperature, followed by rpm, then lap time.

A number of different sensors, or channels, can be installed on your kart. Some are required to ensure proper engine performance while others are more advanced and can be used to evaluate driver performance. Keep it simple when it comes to data acquisition. Four main categories of data acquisition sensors are important to tuning your kart and helping improve driving performance: lap times, miles per hour, temperature, and rpm.

For a driver to become faster, the critical and most basic part of data acquisition is accurate lap times. Lap times allow you to gauge your progress throughout the day. Why are consistent and visible lap times so important to becoming a better driver? It's all about training your brain. Every lap, your brain thinks things like, "that feels good" or "that feels slow." By having lap times, you can train yourself to associate a "good feeling" with a faster lap time. Without accurate real-time feedback,

Drivers can choose from a wide range of sensors that will track information required to properly tune their kart. This engine speed, or rpm, sensor is mounted to the spark slug wire. *Sean Buur*

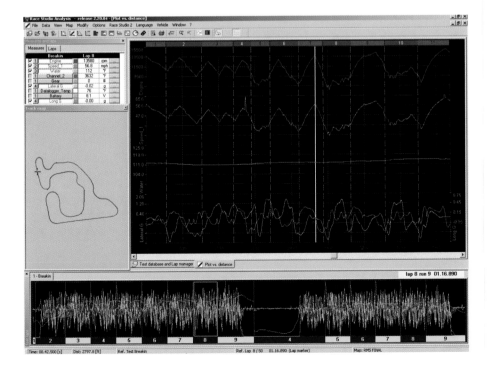

This is what a typical data download to a laptop computer looks like. By using special analysis software from a data acquisition system equipped with track mapping capabilities, the software can actual draw the track layout. *Sean Buur*

Most front sprockets are made of steel and will last a long time. Be sure to get the proper chain to fit the sprockets on your kart. *Sean Buur*

The rear sprocket on most two- and four-cycle karts is made from aluminum. This helps the axle spin faster because it has less weight resistance. Four-cycle karts use the split style (left), while two-cycle karts use the solid type. *Sean Buur*

you may feel good, but you may actually be going slower.

There are two different ways to measure lap times. The first is a beacon, a two-part system requiring the beacon itself and a beacon sensor on the kart. The beacon sensor picks up the signal from the beacon, located trackside. The sensor needs to be mounted with a clear line of sight to the beacon and needs to be at the same height as the beacon to

ensure an accurate reading. The beacon is mounted trackside to transmit a signal as the kart passes, which the sensor picks up to track lap time. It is generally mounted on a tripod, providing the necessary height adjustment, and has different settings so it can function for different karts on the track. The other method uses a magnetic strip embedded in the track, and a sensor is mounted on the floorpan pointing down to the ground. As you pass over the strip, the sensor recognizes it and a lap time is marked.

The other sensor that can really make a difference to any kart racer measures rpm, or engine speed, which is important because the engine needs to operate in the proper range to maximize the kart's power output. The rpm reading is also key to setting up the clutch. Unlike the lap-time scenario, a driver can hear and feel the rpm range. As you work to fine-tune your engine, trusting only your gut can lead to problems, because your gut sense may not be accurate, and being off a few hundred rpm can mean a significant difference in lap time. The rpm measurement is taken from the spark plug lead; this sensor uses the pulse of spark from the ignition to the spark plug to read the rpm.

Another important sensor is for wheel speed. Typically, miles per hour

are associated with wheel speed. However, not all basic models come with a wheel speed sensor, as they require a lot of memory. A critical function of a wheel speed sensor is to actually calculate the distance traveled. The distance calculations are used by the software to enable numerous functions, such as track mapping, plot versus distance, and many other vital math channels.

The wheel speed, or miles per hour, can be measured from the front wheel or the rear wheel. Most systems recommend mounting a magnet on the front wheel and attaching the sensor on the spindle area. The magnet passes by the sensor, which picks up the rotation speed of the wheel. When values such as wheel size are programmed into the system, an accurate reading of miles per hour can be obtained. When deciding whether to mount the sensor on the front or rear wheels, keep in mind that the front tires will not get the wheel spin you might see on the rear, which can cause an inaccurate speed reading.

The next key sensor to have on your kart measures engine temperature, which can be taken from the top of the cylinder at the spark plug in or a waterline. Another is the EGT (exhaust gas temperature) sensor mounted on the exhaust header reads the temperature of the exhaust gases as they leave the combustion chamber. Most basic systems only allow for one temperature sensor. If your data-logging system allows for two temperature sensors, then add the EGT sensor as it is an excellent guide to tuning your engine.

With data acquisition installed on the kart, the workload on driver and crew increases. While the tuner may be working on the kart, the driver can evaluate the information and begin to formulate a plan. Having accurate data allows you to track your progress after the race day is complete so you can begin to think about changes before your next race.

Driveline

Gearing is important to overall lap times and to top speed in all forms of kart racing. The only way to change gear ratios comes from the drive sprockets. Finding the right gearing is an exercise in trial and error. A data-acquisition system will help show how changes affect lap times and engine performance. Gearing is specific to each track layout and must be tuned to work with your engine setup. Gearing affects the speed at every rpm range, so it's important that these match to ensure maximum performance. Remember, you can't create horsepower by altering your gearing setup. However, you can apply your available horsepower in the best possible way with proper testing and careful planning.

The basic principle of gear ratios is quite simple. The ratio is based on comparing the number of turns the front sprocket makes versus the rear sprocket. A lower ratio—the front gear and the rear gear being close in size—creates high speed with low torque. With a higher ratio—the gears being much different in size—there is more torque, but less top-end speed is produced. With a kart, you are always looking to set the gearing for the maximum top speed, while making sure that the entire rpm range has adequate pull off the corners.

GEAR ALIGNMENT

To change the rear gears, loosen the engine mount bolts and pull the engine back a couple of inches. Loosen both sides and then remove the bolts. Remove the gear. Be sure to clean the area where the gear sat with contact cleaner. Check that the keyway is in

Having accurate data allows you to track your progress after the race day is complete so you can begin to think about changes before your next race.

Finding the right gearing is an exercise in trial and error.

good shape. Place the new gear on the carrier and install the bolts. If you have gears that come split in two pieces, the matching halves are usually marked for correct installation. Make sure you tighten both bolts equally.

When fitting new gears, it's very important that the gears are properly aligned. Eyeballing may not be good enough, and if you're in doubt, a straightedge rule placed on the sides of the gear will provide the proper alignment. Misalignment of front and rear sprockets is a major cause of rapid wear and loss of horsepower. Chains and sprockets should be checked for worn spots, which could indicate misalignment. Misalignment is usually due to not adjusting the rear sprocket carefully.

To check the alignment, put the kart on a stand, spin the rear wheel, and watch how the chain travels along the sprockets. The chain should run on the center of the teeth; it should not run to one side or snake from one side to the other. Place a straightedge along the front and rear gears, keeping clear of any bolts, nuts, or washers. Look for any gaps between the edge and the gear. Move the rear gear hub assembly to the left or right to bring it into alignment.

There are also a number of laser tools that can be used. These units fit over the rear sprocket and point a laser beam forward toward the front sprocket. You can slide the hub from side to side to line up the beam directly with the front gear.

Get in the habit of cleaning your gears before you put them away. Put each one in a Ziplock bag and mark the size on the outside. This makes finding the one you need quick and easy and keeps your gears from banging into each other in storage.

Chain

During use, a chain will stretch—the pins will wear causing extension of the chain. Assume a 2 percent maximum allowable extension for non-O-ring chains. Using a chain that's been stretched more than the above maximum allowance causes the chain to ride up the teeth of the sprocket. This in turn causes damage to the tips of the gear teeth—the force transmitted by the chain is carried entirely through the top of the tooth, rather than the whole tooth—resulting in premature gear wear. Chains are a consumable item on shifter karts. It's a good idea to carry at least one spare chain—it's cheaper to replace a chain than a set of

When using a chain breaker, be sure you remove the pin that allows you to reconnect the ends properly.
Sean Buur

Alignment Specialty Tools

There are a number of specialty tools you can buy to align the sprockets and gears on your kart. In some cases, such as a clutch mounted inboard, you cannot get a straight edge in place to check the alignment. There are a few different laser tools that can be used. These units fit over the rear sprocket and point a laser beam forward, toward the front sprocket. You can slide the rear sprocket carrier hub from side to side to line the beam up directly with the front gear. This tool is quick and easy to use.

There is a great alignment tool that, like the laser tools, uses the rear sprocket as the point of reference. This tool slips over the rear sprocket and points a straight bar forward. You simply loosen the straight bar and move the bar forward until you reach the front gear. You can then slide the rear sprocket carrier hub from side to side to line the bar up directly with the front gear. The trick is to make sure the tool is firmly in place on the rear sprocket to ensure an accurate alignment.

Whichever method you use, straight edge, laser, or alignment bar, make sure your sprocket and gear are in line. This will help them last longer by reducing wear and reduce the chance of your chain popping off.

The chain tension should have about 3/8-inch play. Be sure that when you check the tension, you rotate the rear wheels to see if the chain has a tight spot. *Sean Buur*

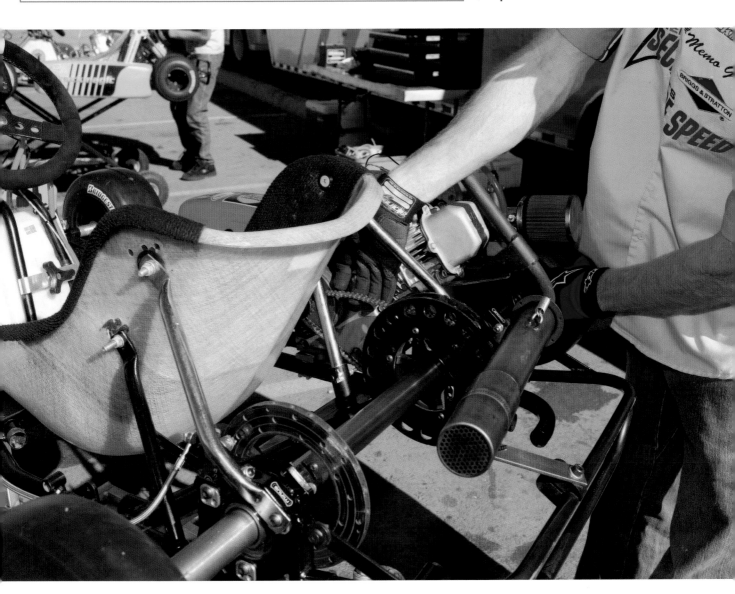

When fitting a new chain,

ensure that the gears

are correctly aligned and

that the chain and gears

are well lubricated.

gears. Also, a new chain runs more smoothly, has less friction, and actually consumes less horsepower.

With a new chain, it is usually necessary to set the proper length to fit your kart. This is done with the help of a chain breaker, which allows you to split a chain quickly and efficiently to add new links or remove a few links to modify the chain length. A chain breaker can ruin your chain if not used properly.

Reducing Wear and Tear

A number of important steps can ensure that your gears and chain not only work well, but also last a long time. Gears should be checked regularly for undue wear. Pointed or stretched teeth are signs of a worn sprocket. A worn sprocket can rob your engine of power and break under use.

Chain tension is a key check as you work on your kart. The chain needs from 3/8 inch to 1/2 inch (9.5 mm to 13 mm) of play for optimal performance. When changing gears or moving the engine, make sure the engine mount is retightened with a minimum of a 3/8 inch (9.5 mm) of slack at the midway point between the sprockets. Having your chain snap can cause expensive damage to your kart. If your chain is damaged, worn, or overstretched, replace it. When fitting a new chain, ensure that the gears are correctly aligned and that the chain and gears are well lubricated.

Make sure the chain guard is in place. This tech item is good protection to you and will keep your kart clean of flying grease. Most karts have a guard that mounts using the PTO holes in the side case. This is an item that may or may not come as part of the kart from your dealer. If your kart is missing a chain guard, there is a quick trick to mount one. Mount a 2-inch strip of plastic about 12 inches long in two places: above the rear sprocket and at

the very bottom. The top can usually be secured with an L-bracket bolted to the bearing cassette. On some karts, the third rail has a tab welded onto it for the chain guard. If yours has one, mount the chain guard to it.

We recommend using a high-quality chain lube like Torco Power Slide Titanium Series. Lube the chain before every run. Be neat about this process by placing a rag or paper towel on the frame under the chain so that any lube that flies past the chain will hit the rag and not get on the frame. Try to wipe up any excess chain lube. Remember to apply chain lube from the inside out, where the chain and the gears meet.

A dirty chain can be cleaned by soaking it in WD-40, which will remove the dirt and the grease in the rollers. You'll need to heavily lubricate the chain after it is cleaned this way. This is only a temporary fix for a chain that's been run through the dirt.

TIRES

Tires have a huge impact on handling and lap times. Keeping this in mind, it's important to make sure that you use tires to their fullest potential. Taking care of your tires will give you an advantage over other competitors. In this section, we will look at how to mount and dismount tires, break-in new tires, and set tire pressures for driving. First, let's take a look at kart tires and rims.

Like a race car, the tires on a kart are tubeless, the air is held inside the tire with a tight seal between the tire bead and the wheel rim. Karts use slicks for dry weather and grooved tires for wet weather. Racing kart tires are low and wide, which allows a kart to have a short sidewall, creating a tire that reacts quickly to driver input.

A kart tire relies on the relationship between heat and air pressure to

perform at its optimum level. Heat is generated by the sidewall flexing and by the contact patch scrubbing on the track surface. As the temperature builds inside the tire, the air temperature goes up and the tire pressure increases, which can also be a factor in heat buildup in a race tire. Tire temperature determines the grip and rolling resistance of the tire.

Tire specifications are stamped into the sidewall. For example an 11x6.50-5 tire is the dimensional size of the tire in inches. The first number, 11, indicates the height of the tire—in this case, 11 inches tall, which is also 11 inches in diameter. The next number, 6.50, indicates the tread width or contact 6.50 inches wide. The last number, 5, designates a rim size of 5 inches.

Most tires will have a directional arrow indicator. It's important to understand that this is the direction the tire should face for acceleration. For karts with only rear brakes, the arrow on both front and rear should point forward, or the normal direction of forward movement. For karts that have front brakes, the front tire direction arrow should face the rear. This is done because a front brake kart loads the front tire opposite to the rear tire, and the tire is designed to absorb these loads for the best performance. Tire compounds vary and are usually determined in the class rules. Clubs will often designate harder compounds, which are designed to last a long time and help keep costs down. Many racing series require a spec tire for all karts.

Kart racing tires come in many sizes and widths. While most kart applications use slick tires, as seen here, some dirt speedway classes have grooves in the tire for better grip. The tire on the left is brand new, while the tire on the right has been used.
Sean Buur

A kart tire relies on the relationship between heat and air pressure to perform at its optimum level.

Kart wheels can be made from aluminum or magnesium. Aluminum wheels tend to hold less heat than magnesium wheels, keeping tire temperatures lower. *Sean Buur*

Different rim materials

handle heat buildup in

different ways.

Rims are also a key component of the wheel assembly. They can be made from stamped aluminum, machined from billet stock, or cast from magnesium. The high amount of grip generated by karts puts a tremendous strain on the rims. Balancing weight and strength is a big factor, as rim failure will put you out of the race. As mentioned before, heat plays a big role in tire performance. Different rim materials handle heat buildup in different ways. Also, some rims are designed to be stiffer than others and this can have an effect on kart handling. A stiffer or softer rim will have an effect similar to a stiffer or softer axle. The lower the grip or smoother the track, the stiffer a rim you might want; the higher the grip or the bumpier the track, the softer the rim you might

choose. All karts use a three-bolt pattern for mounting rear rims.

Choosing the Right Pressure

New tires need a little break-in time before they reach optimum grip levels. New tires have a slick surface to keep the rubber fresh and protect them from contaminants. This, along with a coating of mold release, makes the outer surface of the tire very slippery, making the first few turns on your new tires very slick. Try not to excessively slide the kart or spin the wheels until the grip level rises. Every heat cycle on tires makes them harder, so bring the temperature up slowly to ensure proper break-in. Too much heat too fast can shorten the life of the tires.

Once you've scrubbed your tires and brought them up to temperature,

Set your cold pressure before you go out onto the track. The front tires should be 1 to 1¹/₂ pounds less than the rear tires. *Sean Buur*

pull into the pits and check your tire pressures while they're hot. Because the tire pressure is so important to performance, an accurate gauge is essential. The maximum pressure of kart tires is usually below 40 psi and the minimum can be as low as just a couple of pounds. You need a gauge that has a range from 0 to 40 psi and is accurate enough to read pound increments.

Set the tire pressures hot, because that's the temperature the tires operate at on the track. It's also important to note the differences between your starting cold and your racing hot tire pressures. Proper pressure is difficult to generalize because it can vary with driver, chassis, track layout, road surface, weather, and temperature. Hot pressures come in 2 to 3 psi higher than cold. Make adjustments to your cold pressure to ensure that you hit the optimum hot pressure at the right time. Consult your kart shop for desired operating pressures for your tires. Outside temperature change has a big impact on tire pressure; the general rule is to raise pressure during the cool part of the day. This decreases the contact patch and generates more heat quicker. As the day warms up (around noon), you may have to decrease the pressure by 1 to 3 psi to stay at your optimal hot tire pressure.

You should know your race tire pressure from practice. Race pressure lets you run at your optimum lap time for enough laps to last the race. Tire pressure that's too high builds up too

Check air pressure as soon as you come off the track to get hot tire pressures. *Sean Buur*

It is possible to adjust tire pressures to help fix a handling problem, as air pressure has a big effect on the stability of your kart.

much heat too quickly and causes the tires to lose grip. Low starting pressure causes the tires to lack grip at the beginning of the race. You can run mock races in practice to find the right starting pressure, making sure you always check the pressure while the tires are hot. Check the pressures when the tires have cooled down and make a note of both the hot and cold pressures in your logbook.

It is possible to adjust tire pressures to help fix a handling problem, as air pressure has a big effect on the stability of your kart. For excessive hopping, try adding slightly more tire pressure to settle the kart down. Adding a substantial amount of tire pressure will take away grip from that tire. If you have a push, adding more pressure in the rear will take away grip and give the kart a better balance. Never use this as a long-term fix to a problem, though. The goal is to get the tires to work at their maximum grip level and then tune the kart handling to that grip. Only use tire pressures to help handling when fine-tuning is your goal.

Also watch for the tire to shred or get small cuts or splits in the surface. This may be a sign that the tire is overheated. The tire should have a pebbled look to it. If the tire overheats even once, it will suffer a significant amount of deterioration in grip next time you run.

MAINTENANCE

One of the more important things you can do for your kart is to keep it clean—a clean kart is a happy kart and a happy kart is a fast kart—the idea being that anything mechanical operates better when properly maintained and cleaned. This eliminates possible problems and helps you discover loose bolts or damaged parts before they become a problem and lose you a race.

Start by blowing off all the dirt and dust you can. Be careful when using compressed air; always wear safety glasses when using an air hose. Next, take a rag and lightly coat it with WD-40; this will help cut through the grease and grime on your kart and help to keep rust from forming on any bare metal surfaces. Start at the front of the kart, which is usually the cleanest, and work your way back. The chain area is the last spot to clean because this area contains the most amount of grease.

It's a good idea to remove the wheels and clean the hubs and rims. Use this as an opportunity to check the studs, rims, bolts, and tires for damage. Don't be afraid to pull off the hubs and give them a quick cleaning, but make sure you take width measurements before you pull them off. Most hub problems come from grit and grease getting in between the hub and the axle, either causing them to slip or be difficult to adjust. Your hubs should move easily when loosened and be solidly in place when tight. Put the wheels back on and tighten the stud bolts firmly.

Another area to keep clean is the rear axle. With a chain and chain lube, this area can be a real mess because grease flies everywhere and then attracts grit. Start with a clean rag and remove as much as possible. Use WD-40 to loosen and remove the stubborn grease on the bearings, axle, and rear gear—using WD-40 will lubricate parts while being cleaned. Clean the entire rear end, including the bumper, frame, bearings, and cassettes, by putting some WD-40 on a rag and wiping the surface. This will make the next cleaning even easier.

Properly working brakes are important and you should take the time to maintain them and check for any problem areas. Start with a dry rag and remove as much dust and grime as possible. Clean in and around the rotor hub and the caliper. Using a good-quality brake cleaner, take the nozzle hose and spray into the brake caliper. This should force out any brake dust or

Don't be afraid to pull off the hubs and give them a quick cleaning, but make sure you take width measurements before you pull them off.

Many karts, especially the dirt Speedway karts, use a foam pre-filter to help keep the dirt out of the engine. Air filters need to be treated with a special oil to ensure they trap the most amount of dirt and still let air into the engine. *Sean Buur*

The steering column support bracket is a friction-fit area and can collect a lot of grit.

track grit. Don't be afraid to use the cleaner, as it dries with no residue, but try not to soak the pad itself.

Another area to keep clean is the engine. Start at the top of the engine using contact cleaner and compressed air. For those areas with heavy grease, a toothbrush along with contact cleaner and compressed air works great for cleaning Just don't go crazy with the contact cleaner, and make sure to keep

away from all painted surfaces. If you have run off course and picked up a lot of dirt, don't forget to remove the tank bolt and clean underneath the fuel tank. The grit in between the floorpan and the fuel tank can act like sandpaper and wear on both the plastic tank bottom and the aluminum surface of the floorpan.

After a race day, you should pull the engine for a more thorough cleaning.

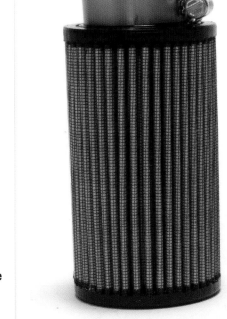

Air filters come in many sizes and shapes. Be sure to get the one that is right for your kart. The filter on the right is the Green air filter used on the Briggs & Stratton World formula Engine. *Sean Buur*

This is a K&N air filter mounted on the Yamaha YF200R1. It is a cloth type filter and uses a nylon pre-filter to trap larger dirt particles before they reach the filter. *Sean Buur*

Remove the engine and place it on your bench. When you remove the exhaust pipe and carburetor, do not forget to place a clean shop towel or cloth into the exhaust port and the intake flange to make sure nothing gets into the engine while you're cleaning it. Wipe off all surfaces and make sure all the electronic parts are cleaned. Wipe off the chassis where the engine mount sits, and wipe off the side of the seat—this usually gets covered in grime. Clean the engine mount thoroughly, including the brackets that go underneath. You want a nice, clean contact between the engine mount and the chassis to ensure the engine doesn't move.

Another part that gets overlooked is the steering column support bracket. This is a friction-fit area and can collect a lot of grit. Remove the bracket bolt and slip the bracket up the steering shaft. Wipe off the column and put it back in place with a little WD-40 for good measure. Make sure to wait a few minutes before reinstalling so all of the WD-40 can run through.

The finishing touch to a clean kart is the bodywork. If the bodywork is relatively clean, the process is simple. Take a clean rag and spray it and the bodywork with WD-40. WD-40 works great to loosen all the stained grease and will not smear and ruin your stickers—never use brake or contact cleaner. Not only will they ruin your stickers, they will also dry out and fade your bodywork. After the bodywork is free of all grease, take another clean rag and clean with a formula like Simple Green. This will give the plastic that nongreasy look and help keep dust and dirt from building up on the surface.

Never use brake or contact cleaner to clean bodywork—they'll ruin your stickers and dry out and fade your bodywork.

Chapter 6

KART TUNING

A typical four-cycle sprint kart setup. Sprint karting is the most popular form of karting in the world and the one most commonly referred to when people think about karting.
Sean Buur

Tuning your kart involves working on many different parts, including the chassis, tires, clutch, and engine. All of these components work together to maximize your kart's performance. Tuning is a constant process that changes with different tracks and as track conditions change throughout the day. It's important that you keep very detailed notes, which will serve as a baseline as you make changes and also as a reference should you return to that track.

STARTING YOUR KART

Before you fire up the engine—and after you've gone through routine checks—you must add fluids to your kart. Make sure you use the manufacturer's recommended fluids and specified amounts. Check with your local dealer or engine builder if you're not sure what fluids your kart requires.

With four-cycle engines there is no need to mix oil and gas. The crankcase of the engine will take any 30-weight oil; some engine builders recommend very thin oils. And in most cases, your four-cycle engine will run with regular-grade pump gas.

A two-cycle engine needs a mix of fuel and oil together before starting. Make sure you get the recommended fuel/oil mixture from your engine builder. Mixing cans are available that allow you to mix the oil and fuel properly and accurately.

It's a good idea to fill the fuel system before starting the engine. On motors with a secondary fuel tank, after putting fuel in the primary tank, take the fuel line off the carburetor and aim it

into the gas can. Blow into the gas tank vent line until fuel flows through the fuel line and into your gas jug. Now that the fuel line is full, reattach it to the carburetor. Filling the line with fuel will keep you from turning the motor over excessively to start it. Make sure you put a small tye wrap over the fuel line to keep it secure on the carburetor nipple.

Have a friend stand at the front of the kart applying light throttle, approximately an eighth of full power. Put the starter gun into the nut or pull the starter cord and turn the engine over. On a TAG engine, press the start button. Once the engine starts, run it at a low rpm until it warms up. When warming up the motor, vary the throttle to keep the engine from loading up. If the idle is set properly, the engine should idle nicely at about 500 to 600 rpm. If not, adjust the carburetor idle by

When warming up the motor, vary the throttle to keep the engine from loading up on fuel.

Track Width

Track change refers to widening or narrowing the front or rear wheels to affect kart handling. Changing front or rear track width will effectively shift grip from one end to the other. Here are a couple of quick examples. If you move the rear wheels out, you reduce rear wheel hop. If you move the rear wheels in it helps the kart turn better because the kart unloads because the kart unloads the inside wheel more.

Rear track changes are made on the axle. All rear wheels are attached to the axle using hubs that slide over the axle and clamp tightly in place. Move the hubs out to widen track width, and closer together to narrow it. Keep in mind that some rear hubs have a lip on them that prevents the hub from sliding all the way past the end of the axle.

Front track width change is done in two different ways. Most karts use a spindle or a hub system on the front. Both systems use spacers between the bearing and the inside of the spindle. These spacers can be moved from the inside to the outside to bring the wheels closer together, from the outside to the inside to move the wheels further apart. On shifter karts with front brakes, there is a hub that slides from side to side to change the track width. Moving the wheels closer together creates less weight jacking while moving them further apart creates more weight jacking and a more responsive front end.

---

adjusting the cable or the idle screw. This can be done while the engine is off, or running—just be careful if you do it while running.

First Laps

When you come in from your first session, you need to check some basic things. These basic checks should become habit after every on-track session. Have your charts ready so you can quickly write down your observations.

The first thing to check is tire pressure. It is *critical* to take pressure readings immediately to get accurate hot tire pressures. Compare these tire pressure readings to the cold pressure settings when you went out. Each tire should have increased from 2 to 3 psi. Check the tires for any cuts or marks that may indicate a problem.

It's important to have a quick look at all of your kart's components. Make sure all the brackets are still tight and that there are no loose nuts or bolts. Check to see if there are any fuel leaks; look for fuel under the seat and on the back of the kart. Check all lines for cuts, rubbing, or chaffing. We recommend that all fuel lines be secured with a small tye wrap to keep them from backing off their nipples.

Next, pull the spark plug and check for color. It should be light brown, almost coffee colored, in the middle porcelain area, and black on the outer metal ring around the porcelain. If the color is drastically different, consider a jetting change.

After the four-cycle engine has cooled, slowly remove the oil drain plug, usually located at the front of the engine. Extreme caution should be taken when removing the oil drain plug to avoid injury from hot oil. Try to let the oil flow into a measuring cup to make sure the level is not down; if the level is down, the system is leaking. Let the oil flow through your fingers and feel for any particles or metal shavings. Put the plug back in carefully and *do not* overtighten.

Finally, check the chain tension. A new chain will stretch as it breaks in. If there is more than 3/8 inch (9.5 mm) play, adjust the chain as outlined earlier. As you move the engine forward, make sure you don't pull on any electrical, water, or fuel lines.

Be sure to write down any notes as you run through the post-session review.

It is critical to take pressure readings immediately to get accurate hot tire pressures.

This information will be very valuable as you begin to fine-tune your kart.

KART CLUTCH 101

The centrifugal, or single-speed, clutch is truly an amazing engineering marvel. Most often the clutch is the hardest working and most ignored part of a kart. No matter how strong your engine is, or how well your chassis is set up, if the clutch isn't working properly, you will not be competitive. The clutch transfers the torque and power from the engine to the rear sprocket. You can lose a great deal of horsepower between the crankshaft and the rear axle sprocket if you don't keep your clutch properly tuned and in good shape.

The clutch allows the engine to freewheel (non-engaged state) for starting and idling. This freewheeling is maintained up to some preplanned slip point when the clutch achieves lockup and drive occurs. A clutch harnesses the power of centrifugal force and friction to drive the kart forward. If you

think about it, a kart clutch is just the opposite of brakes. We use the force created through the master cylinder and the friction of pads on the brake rotor to slow us down. A clutch uses force and friction to speed the kart up. Clutch lockup is achieved by the centrifugal force of rotation and torque overcoming the preload tension of the springs. When rpm reaches a level of force that engages the mechanism, the clutch is said to lock up. After the clutch has locked up, the torque is transferred to the rear axle, into the tires, and down the track you go.

A number of different styles and types of clutches are available. The two main types are disc and drum. The disc clutch resembles disc brakes for a car, and the drum-style clutch resembles drum brakes. Shoes covered in brake material or made of steel push on the drum to create friction and move the kart. A disc clutch can transmit more horsepower with less mass than a drum-style clutch and has more adjustment,

SLIPPING THE CLUTCH

Slipping the clutch refers to partially engaging the clutch lever to partially engage the clutch. This is done at a standing start to avoid excessive wheel spin as the power is applied, while not using all available power.

The clutch is the hardest working and most ignored part of a kart.

The drum clutch is much larger and heavier than most disc clutches. However, the disc clutch requires more maintenance. *Sean Buur*

This is a Horstman wet clutch. "Wet" refers to the fact that the discs are housed inside a casing filled with oil. These clutches were popular in the 1980s. *Sean Buur*

The drum-style clutch is user friendly and handles the bottom-end torque well.

making use of multiple discs to compensate for weight. The drum-style clutch is more often seen in four-cycle applications because it's more user friendly and handles the bottom-end torque well. Four-cycle racing only uses the dry clutch, while some two-cycle classes run a wet clutch. Choosing the right clutch is both simple and complex. In most four-cycle kart-racing classes use of specific clutches are not designated. Look at the other drivers in your class to get a good idea of the right clutch for your class. Always check with your local kart shop, engine builder, and clutch manufacturer to ensure you get the clutch that will work best for you.

Disc Clutches

In general, the disc clutch is lighter than the drum clutch and has more tuning options. A disc clutch has a hub that's connected to the crankshaft and spins with the engine. Connected to this hub is a series of levers and compression springs. The springs hold the pressure plate, and the levers push against the pressure plate. Mounted on the same shaft, a drum spins freely and has the drive sprocket attached. The

friction discs connect to the drum with outer lugs that fit into the channels of the drum.

So, for a disc clutch, the number of discs used is determined by the driver. The general rule is that as weight is added—going from junior to medium to heavy classes—discs need to be added. With more mass to move, more friction is required to move you and your kart forward. By adding more friction discs, you increase the amount of friction surface area. Keep in mind that a clutch with fewer discs is not faster than one with more discs and vice versa.

As engine rpm increases, the outward force of the spinning hub drives the levers away from the center. The levers push the pressure plate against a series of friction discs that engage the outer drum. The drum begins to spin and drives the gear that moves the kart forward. The basic engagement speed of the clutch is predetermined by the levers that pivot in response to centrifugal force. The pivoting of the levers is restrained by the compression springs. A variety of engagement points, or stall speeds, can be obtained by adjusting the spring tension. We will look at the theory and setting of stall speed later on.

Finally, we will check the air gap. The air gap is the space between the friction plates and the pressure plate, and is adjustable on all disc clutches. This gap must be set correctly to ensure the clutch works properly and spins freely at idle. If there is too much gap, the clutch will be slow to engage. If the air gap is too small, it will create heat as the friction disc rubs against the pressure plate. As they rub they expand with the heat and begin to rub even more.

The factory preset air gap should be fine for most conditions. The air gap will need to be adjusted as the friction plates wear and as race conditions change. For multiple-disc clutches, a selection of floaters is available from 0.040 inch thick to 0.060 inch thick in increments of 0.005 inch. The factory air gap is 0.050 inch with normal tolerance of +/- 0.005 inch. When air density is low, increase the air gap by 0.005 inch. Do not exceed the limits prescribed by your clutch manufacturer.

Drum Clutches

The drum clutch is far simpler than the disc clutch. A drum clutch, like a disc clutch, has a hub that's connected to the crankshaft and spins with the engine. Connected to this hub is a series of springs. The springs hold the shoes in place. There are usually three shoes, with three springs on each shoe. In some applications there are two shoes that are held at each end by a spring. Mounted on the same shaft, a drum spins freely and has the drive sprocket attached. In terms of drum clutches, there is no difference in size of the drum.

As engine rpm increases, the outward force of the spinning hub drives the shoes away from the center, pushing the shoes outward against the drum. The drum begins to spin and drives the gear that moves the kart forward. The springs, shoes, and small

The air gap must be set correctly to ensure the clutch works properly and spins freely at idle.

The disc clutch uses a series of small levers that rotate outward as the clutch spins. These levers apply pressure to a pressure plate that engages the drive disc. *Sean Buur*

The drum clutch uses shoes that rotate outward as the clutch spins. These shoes push out against the drum lining, engaging the drum which drives the kart. *Bernd Fuchs*

weights that respond to centrifugal force predetermine the basic engagement speed of the clutch. A variety of engagement points, or stall speeds, can be obtained by adjusting the springs or shoes or weights.

Installation

When mounting a clutch to your engine, first make sure the keyway fits properly and isn't sloppy. Always apply a very thin coat of good-quality grease to the crankshaft before you install the

FOUR-CYCLE CLUTCH INSTALLATION

On a four-cycle kart engine you can mount the clutch both inboard (sprocket beside the motor) and outboard (sprocket away from the engine). All the four-cycle engines talked about in this book are left or inside drive. This positions the clutch between the seat and the engine. However, this produces some problems, especially for larger drivers trying to mount their seat. The reason we can mount both inboard and outboard is the fact that four-cycle engines use a 3/4-inch crankshaft, which can take the added pressure of

the sprocket being mounted on the end. The crankshaft has a standard key way. Also most two-cycle engines used in clutch drive formats have a tapered end on the crankshaft, unlike the four-cycle engines where the crankshaft is the same diameter across the entire length. The four-cycle crankshaft makes it easy to mount inside or outside. When mounting outboard, you will need extra spacers to keep the clutch arms from hitting the side case of the engine. Check with your clutch manufacturer before mounting.

clutch. Too much and it can work its way into the clutch shoes or discs. The idea is to keep the two metal surfaces free of rust and allow the clutch to move freely.

With a disc clutch, you want to check the endplay, or space between the clutch and the inside shoulder of the crankshaft. Endplay is an important measure to make sure the clutch performs well. This is different for two- and four-cycle engines. For two-cycle the clutch needs to fit the taper of the crankshaft. The cltuch needs to be fairly tight. When the clutch is tightened securely to the shaft you should be able to spin the drum freely. If the drum doesn't spin freely, remove the clutch and replace the spacer with a new spacer of appropriate width. A

temporary solution would be to grind some material off the original spacer. The recommended minimum clearance is 0.005 inch and the maximum is 0.015 inch. If you have over 0.015-inch clearance, the clutch may not be properly seated all the way onto the shaft.

For a four-cycle engine you want to allow the clutch to float freely on the crankshaft by using an extra 8-mm washer in front of the clutch washer. The 8-mm washer's diameter is slightly less than the 3/4-inch shaft, allowing the clutch hub to slip over the washer. You may need to use a couple of washers to give the required play. Make sure the main large washer is on the outside. Tighten the bolt on the shaft, allowing the clutch to float freely. The bolt has a

A typical four-cycle clutch setup with a Honda GX200 engine. The clutch can be mounted inboard or outboard, depending on which side the gear is placed. *Bernd Fuchs*

Endplay is an important measure to make sure the clutch performs well.

Stall Speed

The stall speed is the point where the clutch "locks," providing maximum transfer of power. The term stall is used to refer to the fact that engine rpm will go flat, or stall, for an instant when the clutch fully engages. The clutch doesn't make power; it can only transmit the available torque from the engine to the rear axle. In karting, the clutch is subject to extreme abuse as it is repeatedly required to perform with a controlled slip, which of course creates high heat. The clutch's biggest enemy is heat. A clutch gets overheated, or "smoked," for any number of reasons. The main problem is that the stall-speed adjustment is set above the peak torque of the engine.

Proper stall-speed adjustment will enable your engine to operate within its most efficient power band, which should provide the fastest lap time. The clutch is normally engaged at 200 to 300 rpm before torque peak, rather than at torque peak, allowing the clutch to engage and issue adequate power to drive through the torque peak and rpm range without bogging the engine down. If the clutch engages at torque peak, the clutch will lock and drop off, as there won't be enough power to sustain and carry the engagement forward. The clutch needs to lock up at maximum torque, so, it is very important to engage the clutch at 200 to 300 rpm before torque peak.

Dry clutches perform very well with low maintenance up to 3,500 rpm stall speed. As you increase the stall speed above 3,500 rpm, clutch maintenance also increases. If you operate the clutch above 3,500 rpm, you may need to service the clutch every race weekend. Consult your engine builder or the manufacturer of your clutch for precise stall-speed settings.

A tachometer is needed to set the stall-speed range for optimum performance. The correct procedure is to look at the tack just as you go to full throttle on the tightest corner of the racetrack. This will give you the best reading to set your clutch.

1/2-inch head so be careful; use some thread lock to keep it in place.

The inside edge of the crankshaft next to the engine is slightly rounded. If you tighten the clutch drum against it you can crack the hub, which is why the drum is tightened against the washers, letting the clutch float. This is the same for disc or drum, inboard or outboard. For a disc clutch you will need a special spacer if mounting outboard. The spacer will slide on first and keep the levers away from the side of the engine. For drum clutches, there is no difference whether you mount it inboard or outboard.

FINDING THE RIGHT BALANCE

Putting your kart on scales is perhaps the most important thing you can do to ensure proper handling. The first thing to check is that all tires are of equal circumference side to side, and that all chassis settings, such as caster and camber, are also symmetrical from side to side. Next, align the front end and lock the steering nut to keep the steering from moving during the scaling process. The steering can be locked by using a Vise-Grips locked onto the steering shaft while resting it against the frame.

The most basic approach is to use four bathroom scales (one for each tire)

set on level ground. Unless you have a surface that's perfectly flat, after putting the kart one direction, pick it up and rotate it 180 degrees. Then take the average reading of each scale to get the actual reading for every tire. The best type of scales are the electronic ones with individual leveling pads. Putting your kart on the scales is really the final touch after you've set up the chassis, mounted the seat, and installed the engine. Weighing and balancing the kart ensures that proper overall weight and ideal weight distribution is achieved. As a result, the kart has the potential to perform to its optimal level. With scaling and balancing, all the work you've done to correctly assemble your kart comes together.

Before you begin to race, make sure that the weight is properly distributed to the four corners of the kart. The

weight balancing, or scaling process, is actually measuring the amount of weight that each tire is bearing. Scaling will also provide some telltale signs that your setup is not accurate or your chassis is bent.

Why is kart balancing so important to overall performance? We learned that a kart must shift weight from the inside rear tire to the outside rear tire to efficiently turn through a corner. This weight transfer is helped by the geometry of the kart's front and the flex of the chassis. In order to accomplish this weight transfer evenly and effectively, we need to begin with a kart that's properly balanced, a kart with even overall weight distribution.

We learned on seat setup, the overall design of a chassis is meant to help compensate for the weight of the engine by placing the seat to the left of

A close-up shot of a two-cycle clutch mounted on a KT 100. Because the crankshaft is much smaller in a two-cycle than a four-cycle, the clutch can also be smaller. *Bernd Fuchs*

Weighing and balancing the kart ensures that proper overall weight and ideal weight distribution is achieved.

Memo Gidley scales his signature-series Trackmagic shifter kart. It is important to wear all your equipment while scaling your kart to ensure an accurate reading. *Jeff Deskins*

Do not use lead shot on your frame to increase the weight.

center. Proper seat installation may result in almost perfect weight distribution before any extra weight is added to the kart. The other benefit of scaling your kart is so you can get a clear understanding of exactly how much the kart weighs with the driver. You can then determine how much weight needs to be added to meet class weight minimums.

When you add weight to a kart for balancing, it's important to understand some basic physics. Remember, an object will stay in motion until acted upon. For this reason, we recommend that the weight be placed as close to the center of the mass as possible, while still achieving the desired equal corner weights. Weight added outside this range requires more

energy to change its direction. Imagine a huge lead weight bolted on the rear bumper. As you enter a turn, the chunk of lead still wants to go straight. Some of the grip must now be used to change its direction. Once you get it moving in the right direction, you have to stop it from swinging and changing its direction again. This type of pendulum effect has a big impact on kart handling.

When placing lead on your kart, it's best to start by bolting it on the seat. The best place to put it is on the left or backside of your seat, depending on your readings. Rubber-covered scuba-diving weights work well for this. They come in convenient increments, look good, and are easy to handle. Do not use lead shot on your frame to increase the weight. The shot has a tendency to shift and can make the frame rails stiffer, which may adversely affect handling.

Once final weight placement is determined, secure all weight properly. The weights can be frame-mounted with proper mounting brackets, and the hardware will need to be at least 5/16-inch grade 5 or better, or 8.8 M8 bolts of the appropriate length. Be sure to cross drill and safety wire or safety clip each one. Most sanctioning bodies require double nutting of the ballast as well. Be sure to consult your rule book. Not securing your weight properly has the potential to cause injury and equipment damage and can lead to disqualification from a race.

Balancing your kart is not a one-time process, and should be done regularly.

This is especially true if you make a major change, such as a new seat. A set of kart scales is a significant investment. You may choose to share the cost and use of the scales with a couple of friends.

CHANGES AND ADJUSTMENTS
First look at the basics when you are thinking of handling changes. Ask yourself some questions. Is the front-end slow (push) turning in or too quick (loose)? Did the rear tire lift at all or too much? Does the front-end jacking too much weight, or not enough, cause this? Is the kart transition from turning at the apex to accelerating down the straight smooth and easy to drive? When did the rear tire feel like it began to settle down? Is the kart hopping?

Balancing your kart is not a one-time process, and should be done regularly.

Lead weights can be added to your kart to increase overall weight. All weight added needs to be secured so it doesn't fall off. *Jeff Deskins*

Camber can affect understeer through the size of the contact patch.

The wider the front end, the more the tire will drop, causing more weight-jacking effect.

Understeer

Understeer, also referred to as push, is most often seen as poor corner turn in. The main cause of understeer is that the inside rear tire is not picking up and the kart has to struggle to turn. If this is the problem, it can be fixed. We know that anything that we do to increase the weight jacking effect will help lift up the inside rear tire. The most common change is increasing the caster, which will increase weight jacking.

The other way to correct understeer is camber. Camber can affect understeer through the size of the contact patch. At most tracks there will be plenty of front tires with substantial wear on the inside edge, yet virtually no wear on the outside. This is due to the camber settings asking only a small part of the tire to do any work. As a result,

this smaller tire footprint will have a tendency to overheat, especially in hot conditions, contributing to premature tire wear and understeer.

Camber also affects understeer in its ability to jack weight. It's common for most karts to come with zero camber. Because the profile of a front tire is generally flat across the top, zero camber is a good trade-off between contact patch and weight jacking. The more positive camber you induce, the more the outside edge of the tire pushes down in turning and the more weight jacking you have.

The other change that will affect weight jacking and push is the front track width. Put your kart on a stand and turn the wheels. Notice that the outside wheel drops down. Making the front end wider will move it farther from the pivot point. In other words,

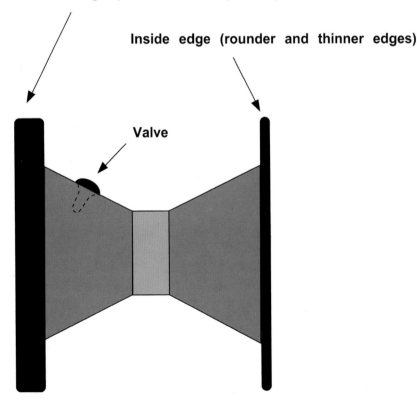

Outside edge (wider and sharper edges)

Inside edge (rounder and thinner edges)

Valve

This is the difference between the inside and the outside of the wheel. Always mount from the inside of the wheel, as the lip is smaller.
Craig Ketchen

the wider the front end, the more the tire will drop, causing more weight-jacking effect. The other area to help with push is changing the center of gravity by picking up the inside rear tire. This can be done in many ways. The first one is raising the seat up or tilting it forward. Either of these will raise the weight, which gives the cornering forces more leverage to pick up the tire. Other options to accomplish similar characteristics include moving your lead up or raising the rear ride height.

And finally, another option to change push is to narrow the rear track width. Imagine a triangle using the driver's head and both rear tires as points of intersection. The narrower you make the rear tires, the steeper you make the sides of the triangle. The steeper the triangle, the higher the center of gravity and the more the kart tends to pick up. So, what happens if you go too far with these changes?

Oversteer

The most common cause of oversteer is the kart jacking too much weight. When this happens, the inside rear tire picks up too much, which makes the front end darty and the kart loose. The other clue that this may be happening is if you have excessive hop during turn in. Turn-in hop is created from the inside rear tire picking up and slamming back down hard.

How do you fix this problem? It's really the opposite of fixing understeer, mentioned above. To make the kart jack less weight, you want to reduce the front-end geometry. Things like less caster, less positive camber, and narrower front-wheel width will fix a kart that's darty and/or loose. Changes for less hop can include lowering the seat, moving down your lead, dropping the rear ride height, or widening the rear tire width.

MOUNTING KART TIRES

Anyone who has ever tried to mount a tire on a one-piece wheel rim will agree that it can be a daunting task. Getting the stiff rubber of the tire bead over the edges of the wheel rim is often exceedingly difficult. With proper technique and a lot of practice you can mount tires quickly and painlessly.

Following the steps outlined will make tire mounting much easier. Don't try to do the tire mounting on a hard surface, like concrete or asphalt, since you might damage the tire or rim. Having a piece of carpet is good, because it's soft enough that neither tire nor rim will be scratched or damaged and it will allow the tire-rim combination to get some grip during the mounting process.

First, identify the smaller edge of the wheel rim. Most often it's the inside of the wheel rim, or the side without the valve. Some types of rims, like Douglas Wheels, seem to have equally sized lips on both sides. However, when you look closely at the edge of the inside lip, you can probably see that the lip is somewhat

Mounting tires is very tricky and can take some time to learn. Memo Gidley has had a lot of experience and can mount a set of four tires in less than two minutes. *Jeff Deskins*

With proper technique and a lot of practice you can mount tires quickly and painlessly.

If you plan on changing tires frequently, you will need a bead breaker. This unit from RLV is great and works on all sizes and styles of rims. *Jeff Deskins*

Be sure to apply plenty of lube all the way around the outside of the tire, making sure not to splash it into the inside.

thinner, and that its edge is more rounded. So, even in the case of equally sized lips, the inside lip is still a little easier to slip the tire over.

Place the tire on the ground and lube the outer edge of the tire and the bottom edge of the rim. Be sure the lube is slippery, can be washed off, and won't damage the rubber. A mild cleaner like Simple Green is best for this. Be sure to apply plenty of lube all the way around the outside of the tire, making sure not to splash it into the inside. The moisture from this fluid will have a negative effect on the amount of tire pressure increase on the track. Keep the Simple Green close by, since you might

need it again later. With lube on the outside of the bead, spin the edge of the rim to coat it in lube.

Now kneel down, with the tire flat on the ground. Press the rim down onto the tire on an angle, so the rim makes contact with the tire bead on two points. Now twist the rim while you apply pressure, trying to get the rim to slip into that part of the tire. During this process, you might find that the tire collapses, turning inside out. Putting pressure on the tire in between your knees while pushing the rim in will help to keep this from happening. You will find you can roll or twist the rim into the tire with your hands.

For the other side of the tire, flip the wheel over so the rim is on the floor. Apply some more lube to the inside edge of the rim using a rag. This will avoid getting too much lube inside the tire. Grip the tire very firmly, putting your whole weight behind it. Eventually it should slip on, just the same as the first bead. You may find that you need to grab each side and roll the bead onto the rim.

If you are new to mounting tires, you may also use tire irons to help with the mounting process. Just like mounting without tire irons, you should start with the smaller side of the rim, usually the inside. With the extra leverage you get with the irons, it's important that you don't force the tire on or off the rim. Too much force on the tire will ruin the bead and possibly damage the rim. The key is to take it slow, be patient, and use a lot of lube.

If your rims have bead locks, now is the time to install them. Make sure they are clean and have a rubber O-ring in good condition. Put them in until they are just past flush. You should be able to pass your finger over the hole and just feel the tip of the bead lock. If you put them in too far, the tire will have difficulty seating. If you don't put them in far enough, the hole can fill with the rubber from the bead itself. Taking extreme care with bead locks is important. Bead locks generally do not have much thread to start with and are prone to leaking and stripping.

Just after you have mounted a tire on a rim, you might notice that there is a gap between the tire bead and the wheel rim. When inflating the tires, it's important to get the seal as tight as possible, or you'll have a difficult time getting the bead to seat. Using a compressor, force air in at such a high rate that it cannot escape from the gap fast enough. The tire will rapidly expand until it reaches the rim, providing the desired seal. The valve

core can resist the fast inflation, so it may be necessary to remove the valve core. A strap or piece of rope wrapped tightly around the outside of the tire will help with the seating process. Wrap the strap in the center of the tread and pull tightly while putting air in the tire. The strap helps to push the beads closer to the rim, making a better seal on the tire bead and rim.

As you inflate the tire, the pressure will grow and the bead will start to slide up the rim. Applying plenty of lube can help reduce the friction between the rubber and rim material. When you apply high pressures (40 or 50 psi), you may exceed the manufacturer's recommendations. Be sure to take all necessary safety precautions. Use a long air chuck to give you some safety distance. We recommended that you put your tires into a safety cage to seat the beads. If you're unsure about seating your tires, see your local dealer.

When a bead seats under high pressure, it can produce a loud metallic-sounding *pop*. Don't be alarmed; that's normal. One bead often seats much earlier than the second bead, so keep increasing the pressure. Eventually, the second bead will seat, again with a loud *pop*. Be careful not to get your fingers between the wheel lip and the tire bead when the bead seats. The pressure is capable of seriously squishing your fingers, so make sure your fingers are nowhere near the tire and rim when you're trying to seat the bead.

Once both beads are seated, check that they have even contact with the lip of the wheel rim. To keep from over-stretching the tire, reduce the air pressure back to the hot pressure. To complete the installation process, tighten the bead locks. Make sure you check the bead locks for air leaks by spraying them with soapy water and looking for bubbles.

When inflating the tires, it's important to get the seal as tight as possible, or you'll have a difficult time getting the bead to seat.

When a bead seats under high pressure, it can produce a loud metallic-sounding pop.

Throw out damaged rims, as they can ruin a good set of tires or fail under pressure.

Removal and Storage

Dismounting old tires can be as much a chore as mounting new tires. Although it's much more difficult to remove a tire without tire irons, it's always preferred to avoid using the irons. Even being very careful, using tire irons will mark the rim, which can damage new tires and make mounting more difficult.

First, to remove tires with tire irons, remove the valve core with the valve core removal tool. Next, break the bead using a bead breaker. There are a number of manual units on the market. Break the bead on the inside first, then the outside or valve stem side. With both beads now off the lip of the rim, place the rim, valve stem side down, on a piece of old carpet. Push one edge of the tire to the narrow middle of the rim.

Take the tire iron and place it on the other side and pull down. Take the other iron and do the same. Be careful, because the tire iron can stretch or mark the bead area. When removing the old tires to be discarded, you don't have to worry about the bead area, but be careful with the rim. With the tire irons in place, try to pull the tire over the rim to about half way. The rest of the tire should pop off. Flip the tire over, and the other edge of the rim can be pulled off by hand.

When removing an old tire without a tire iron, the first step is to break the bead as outlined above. Then, with the inside of the tire, roll the top of the tire inward, making the bottom tire bead extend itself over the rim. Grab the extended bead and slowly work the tire off the rim until the entire bead has been removed over the rim.

Flip the tire and rim over and angle the rim into the carpet while putting pressure on the top of the rim with your left hand. Take your right hand and use your palm to slowly work the outside bead over the inside surface of the rim.

Although this technique takes a little practice, it will keep your rims free of marks from using tire irons.

Before using the rim again, check for dents, cracks, and bends. File off any burrs or marks, especially on the lip where the tire bead makes contact. If you have magnesium rims, check for cracks. Throw out damaged rims, as they can ruin a good set of tires or fail under pressure. Clean the rim with contact or brake cleaner. Make sure you remove any rubber that's stuck to the bead seating area. Rims should be stored in a safe place to avoid being banged around. Small nicks and marks on the lip can cut tires when mounting. It is important to wrap your tires after each use.

Taking care of your tires off the track is very often overlooked. Once you've run your tires you've broken the outer seal. This seal keeps the rubber fresh and protects the surface against contaminants like gas, oil, and cleaners.

You need to wrap your tires in plastic wrap and put them in a dark bag or a rack in your trailer. This will keep the environment and sunlight from drying out and hardening the rubber. This is especially important for club racers who use a hard-compound tire that is raced on more than once. Also, this is good for race tires that can be used for practice. Following these simple rules will help to keep tire rubber soft and even help to extend the life of your tires.

PERFORMANCE TUNING
Air Density

Air density, or the relative weight of the air, is the combination of three elements: barometric pressure, air temperature, and humidity. Air density is generally highest at sea level because the barometric pressure is high and the temperature is low. A good example is a cold and sunny winter day. On the other hand, air density will be lowest at a high elevation, where the barometric pressure is generally low and the temperature is high. The amount of water vapor is measured by humidity, which is the least significant factor when evaluating air density.

The most common way to measure air density is with an air-density gauge. Why is air density important? With each intake stroke of the engine, the exact same volume of air is drawn, but the density or weight of that volume of air can vary greatly from day to day, and even hour to hour. For example, at high elevations engines take in less air, so the engine needs less fuel to maintain the desired air/fuel mixture. So, if the density increases and the amount of fuel is not increased, the mixture will be lean, which can lead to a loss of power or worse, a seized piston. Conversely, if the density decreases and you don't reduce fuel volume, the mixture will be rich and the engine won't generate as much horsepower.

Remember, something else goes down as altitude goes up: horsepower. You can expect to lose as much as *3* percent of your power for every 1,000 feet (304.8 meters) that you rise in altitude. So, what does this mean? Cold air is dense air and dense air requires more fuel (bigger jet). Warm air is thin air and thin air requires less fuel (smaller jet). Air density makes that much difference. Always take constant readings of air density and note other weather conditions such as temperature, clouds, proximity to water, and other meteorological factors to determine proper tuning.

Spark Plug Reading

One of the key characteristics of a spark plug is a property called heat range. All conventional plugs have to stay hot enough to burn away deposits that could build up on the electrodes. This buildup would have the effect of short-circuiting, or fouling, the plug. To be safe, plug temperatures should be between 700 degrees Fahrenheit (371 degrees Celsius) and 1,000 degrees Fahrenheit (537.8 degrees Celsius) over the whole range of operating conditions. It's important to understand that it's the engine that puts heat into the plug and not the reverse. Therefore, a hot plug doesn't make an engine run hotter, and neither does a cold plug make the engine run cooler. Knowing which plugs are hotter or colder than the ones you presently have in your engine is easy if you stay with the same brand. Nearly all plug manufacturers use a numbering system to designate heat range. This information is readily available on their websites.

So how can you tell if you're running the correct heat range? Always ask your engine builder what spark plug they recommend. The spark plug will get hot enough to keep the insulator nose completely clean, with all deposits burned away, but not so hot that the electrodes show signs of overheating. The primary evidence that a plug is overheating can be found on the plug's center electrode. The edges on the tip of the electrode will show signs of being rounded by erosion or melting. Try to use a new plug that's been run for just a few minutes.

The best reading of a spark plug comes from a "plug chop," meaning the engine should be cut at full throttle to accurately read the color of the air/fuel mixture. Your engine will have an idle setting, so when you let off the gas the engine will not stall. To do a plug chop, come in off the track fast without a cool-down lap and immediately cut the engine using the kill switch. Then, remove the spark plug and read exactly what occurred in the combustion chamber at high rpm.

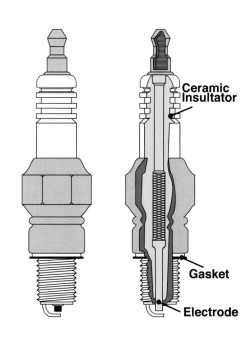

A typical spark plug for two- and four-cycle engines uses a ceramic outer shell and a metallic inner electrode. The spark from the engines ignition travels through this electrode to ignite the compressed air/fuel mixture.
Craig Ketchen

The best reading of a spark plug comes from a "plug chop."

To properly check the spark plug, you need a magnifying glass. Look at the sides of the porcelain insulator; this is the best indication of how rich or lean the engine is running.
Jeff Deskins

Pipe Tuning

All two-stroke engines have an optimum power band. This is the range of rpm in which the maximum power output is achieved. This power band can be moved up and down the rpm range to adapt to the conditions at hand. A two-stroke is a very high-revving engine, with the KT100 engine running just over 15,000 rpm and ICA engines running up to 20,000 rpm. The power band is basically the perfect match of the expansion-chamber shockwave and the combustion stroke—it can feel like an extra kick of power from the engine. When the engine is outside the power band, the rpm range is too low or too high for the combustion stroke and the shockwave to have the proper timing.

The volume of the expansion chamber and the length of the pipe dictate the timing of the shockwave. Therefore, the exhaust port and the expansion chamber can be tuned to put the power band where it will work best given different conditions. The exhaust pipe or expansion chamber for a two-stroke is made up of five specific parts. The part connecting to the cylinder is the head, followed by the diffuser, or diverging cone. The next section is called the dwell, or center section, followed by the baffle, or converging cone, and finally the stinger. The length, angle, and diameter of each of these sections can be adjusted to affect overall engine performance. Many 100-cc air-cooled engine pipes have neither a dwell nor a stinger.

Remember, the pipe needs to be tuned to match the flow of exhaust gases from the exhaust port to the return shockwave in the pipe. The pipe on a two-stroke is truly a magical thing. It has a huge impact on the performance of the engine by harnessing the shockwave or pressure pulse created in the combustion chamber. As this wave travels down the pipe, it moves at the speed of sound and remains unchanged until it enters the diffuser cone. Because two-cycle karts need to have the horsepower made at very high rpm, the header length is quite short.

As the diameter of the pipe increases, the volume of the hot exhaust gas expands, drawing more of the exhaust gases into the pipe. The original wave continues down the pipe and enters the baffle or diffuser. At this point, the main reflective point, the wave, is reflected back toward the engine as a positive pressure wave. This is the magic of a two-stroke. As the original negative wave draws the remaining exhaust gases out of the cylinder on the power stroke it also draws the fresh fuel charge into the pipe. The returning positive wave rams this new air/fuel mixture charge back into the combustion chamber on the combustion stroke.

The length of the pipe and the temperature inside the pipe will control the timing and speed of these waves. So, a longer pipe means a lower power band, which is good for short, tight tracks. A shorter pipe means a higher power band, which is good for faster, longer tracks.

Ignition Timing

Now that you can read what the engine is doing by looking at the plug and piston, you need to dial in your ignition timing. The purpose of ignition timing is to maximize the power created by combustion. Advanced timing causes the spark to happen before top dead

The exhaust pipe for an ICC shifter kart engine. Notice the welding detail done to get the proper shape. This shape helps determine engine performance. *Jeff Deskins*

The purpose of ignition timing is to maximize the power created by combustion.

center (TDC), which is great for low- to mid-rpm, because the mixture has more time to burn and create more pressure in the combustion chamber. The down side is that more heat is created. The impact of more heat is even greater as the rpm rises.

It's best to fire the plug closer to TDC as the rpm rises. The closer the plug fires to TDC, the less pressure and heat rise. The overall advantage is that more heat is put into the pipe and less into the combustion chamber. This has the effect of increasing the rpm range and reducing the possibility of meltdown. It is important to stress that you need to give spark advance very close attention because excessive spark lead is the most frequent cause of detonation. When the spark is advanced too much, the pressure rise in the combustion chamber becomes too great and creates a ping sound. This preignition is a major warning that you've gone too far and seizure is possible.

The timing of the spark is controlled in the constant discharge ignition (CDI). The CDI has a built-in curve that alters the spark timing over the rpm range, allowing for peak power.

Carburetion

With ignition timing under control, you can further fine-tune your engine by tuning the carburetor. Carb tuning is a continuous adjustment because of changing air density.

The first thing the carburetor does is mix air with fuel. The carburetor is always located between the air box and the engine. As the engine draws air in through the carburetor, fuel is metered by a series of needles and jets to mix with the air. Both styles of carburetors use low-speed and high-speed circuits to ensure that the right amount of fuel is available to mix with the air.

The second operation the carburetor performs is controlling the fuel flow to the engine. Butterfly-style carburetors use a "gate" that opens and closes with the throttle pedal. As the gate opens, more fuel is allowed to pass through to the engine. Slide-style carburetors use a slide that moves up and down with the throttle pedal.

Finally, the carburetor can be used to manage changes in air density. The needles and jets determine how much fuel is mixed with the incoming air at various levels of throttle input. In a two-stroke engine, too lean a mixture could have a catastrophic result, because in a two-stroke the lubricating oil is mixed with the fuel—the leaner you run, the less oil will be in the motor to lessen friction. Being too lean will make the piston run hotter, which means more expansion and a tighter piston-to-cylinder clearance. Also, too lean a mixture will starve the cylinder wall and the lower connecting rod bearing of the oil that is in the fuel mixture. When adjusting your carburetor, it's very important to adjust in small steps and to have the help of someone who has the experience to recognize when the mixture is too lean.

You will find that all the different types of jets overlap. For example, when the airscrew stops having an effect, the pilot jet starts controlling the mixture. As in any circuit in the carburetor, as one starts to taper off, the next circuit or jet will start to come into effect. Always start rich and work your way toward lean. Keep changes small and deliberate, and keep an eye on the air density.

Adjusting a carburetor with needles is similar in that you want to start rich and slowly lean down. Also, as is the case with a jet-style carburetor, the high- and low-speed needles overlap and work together. Check with your engine manufacturer for exact

The carburetor can be used to manage changes in air density.

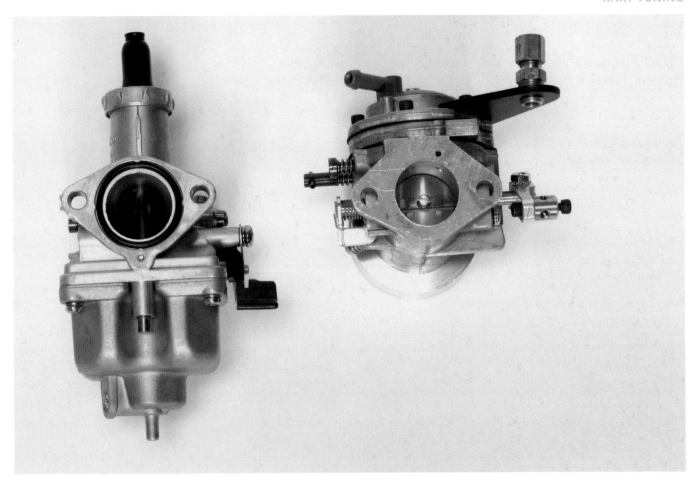

carburetor settings. With these settings, initial throttle response should be good on the low end and ensure that the engine is rich on the high speed. As temperature or track conditions change, slowly adjust needles. Remember, from the baseline setting, if you lean the high speed, you must richen the low speed to keep from running lean.

Never try to jet too close to the perfect mixture until you've taken care of spark advance. The air/fuel mixture that will yield the most power is only slightly richer than the mixture that can cause detonation. You can use the combustion chamber and piston to tell you when there is even slight detonation inside the engine. In a two-stroke engine, look at the top of the piston through the spark plug hole with a bend-a-light to see how the engine is running. Signs of detonation will show as tiny pits on the top of the piston. The piston crown will show detonation sooner than the spark plug will. If the piston is detonating toward the exhaust side, the main jet or high-speed needle is too lean. If the piston is detonating toward the intake side, the pilot jet/needle or low-speed needle is too lean.

A side shot into the opening of a slide-style carburetor on the left and a butterfly style carburetor on the right. Both styles of carburetors are found on two-stroke and four-stroke engines. *Sean Buur*

Signs of detonation will show as tiny pits on the top of the piston.

Chapter 7

DRIVING TECHNIQUES

In all forms of racing the action is close and very fast paced. Here the Comer cadet class gets started for action. *Sean Buur*

Being quick comes from practice through trial and error.

This chapter will help you think about and understand the driving line, race day setup, racing principles, and wet-weather driving. You can't dial in your kart if you're not running the proper racing line. Having a complete understanding of driving-line theory is an area most drivers overlook. Being quick comes from practice through trial and error.

Karts have repeatedly proven to be the most versatile and effective tool for racers looking to improve their driving skills. In fact, most top race car drivers from around the world attribute their success in cars to the lessons learned while driving karts. Karts are such effective teaching tools due to their high levels of grip. The grip level of a kart compares to an F1 or Champ Car, which are considered to be the most

physical race cars in the world. But a kart is much more forgiving if you get into trouble. Karts are high-performance racing machines that you can literally put into the back of your truck and take to the track without a 30-person pit crew. In a kart, smoothness and good technique are rewarded with a fast lap time, while mistakes are punished by seconds lost.

Driving fast on a racetrack is a talent many people think you're born with—you either have it or you don't. Though people are born with certain qualities like fast reaction times, quick decision making and good eyesight—all of which can help drivers go faster—understanding the basic driving techniques, like those in this chapter, is the real key to being fast. Learning proper driving techniques isn't just for the

beginning or novice driver, it's the first step to being the most educated, fastest driver you can be.

BODY POSITIONING

In any type of kart, the driver's movement and input have a major impact on handling. As do body posture and line of vision.

Hand positioning is very personal to each driver, but there is some sound logic to where you place your hands. We recommend that you place your hands in the ten o'clock and two o'clock positions. This provides the best leverage and control. With the amount of grip that current karts can generate, having good leverage is vital. It reduces driver fatigue, and even more important, allows him to be

aggressive with the wheel if the handling is not ideal or if the track has a lot of grip. Make sure that the steering wheel position is not too close or too far in front of you. For sprint kart racing, have a slight bend in your elbows with my hands on the steering wheel at the ten and two o'clock positions. It's amazing that many drivers have never moved their steering wheel to find the right position.

Your hand position is vital to receiving input from the steering wheel, providing much needed feedback from the kart. It's very important to be relaxed in a kart—don't put a death grip on the steering wheel. This uses up energy and reduces your reaction times. Loosen your fingers as you drive down the straights. Not only does this help

You must be comfortable in the seat with hands placed at two and ten o'clock. Your knees will be slightly bent and your feet close to the pedals. *Sean Buur*

Place your hands in the ten o'clock and two o'clock positions.

It is important in any type of kart to have your shoulders parallel to the ground. Try to avoid leaning to the inside of a corner. *Sean Buur*

The apex is the tightest point in any given turn.

relieve arm pump for the occasional driver, but it also reminds more experienced drivers to drive loose, which will help them feel the racetrack better.

Driving posture is an important part of learning to be smooth, fast, and consistent.

Your back should be straight with the seat, your shoulders parallel with the ground. A typical beginner's mistake is to lean into or out of corners. Leaning into or out of corners affects the weight transfer and handling of your kart and makes it harder to be consistent. Keep an upright and strong posture in the seat; let your arms work the steering wheel and your feet work the pedals. If you have to move your body to turn the wheel or push the pedals, you need to make the proper adjustments.

DRIVING-LINE COMPONENTS

"Use the entire track," is a phrase often heard in racing circles. On a track, there are elements that make up a corner—including the entry point, the apex, the exit point, braking and accelerating, which will allow you to do just that: "use the entire track." The basic theory is the same for speedway and for indoor racing, with a few small twists.

The first point is called the turn in. This is where the turn is initiated, where you begin to change direction and steer into the corner. It's critical to get this point right because it stes the tone for the rest of the corner.

The apex is the tightest point, or clipping point, in any given turn. This is where you are the closest to the inner curbing. An apex is not always a point, but can be a stretch of track where you are the tightest to the inside of the turn.

The exit point is where you have released, or straightened out, the steering wheel completely. It's generally found just at the outside edge of the track. This is important because how you come out of a turn determines how fast you will be going down the straightaway or how well you will be set up for the next turn.

As a driver, your first job is to slow down or brake for the turn. You will experience two types of braking situations heading into a corner: threshold braking and trail braking. If you are braking in a straight line, you are attempting to maximize the entire avail-able grip for slowing down. Usually the maximum grip is achieved just before the tires lock up. This is described as threshold braking, or braking at 100 percent of the kart's limit. As you turn into the corner, you need to transfer some of that grip for cornering or face going straight off the track with your tires locked up. This is where trail braking comes into play. Trail braking is the process of letting off the brakes as you enter into the corner so that you can use some of your available grip for cornering. The more you turn into the corner, the more brakes you need to release to have grip for cornering.

As you complete the corner, you need to have some grip available for accel-

The more you turn into the corner, the more brakes you need to release to have grip for cornering.

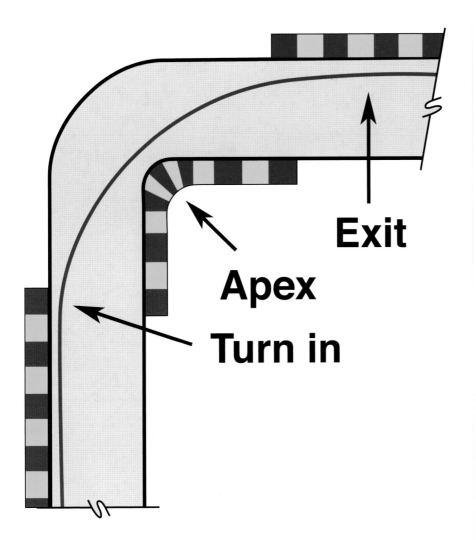

Exit

Apex

Turn in

These are the various parts of a racing line. Finding that line on each corner of the track is key to improving your lap times.
Craig Ketchen

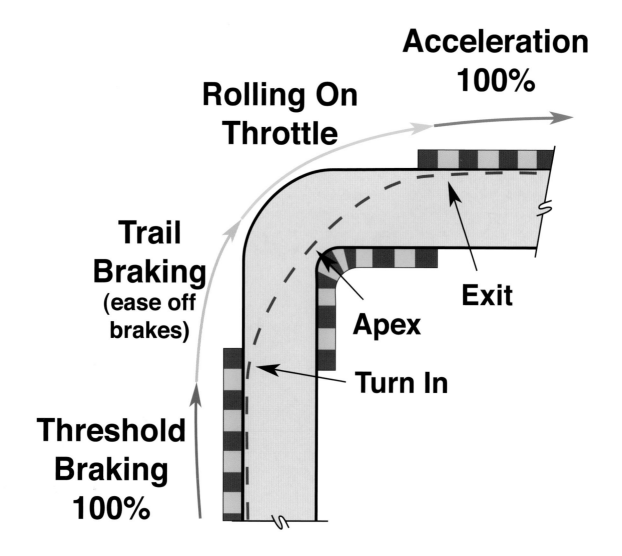

Acceleration 100%

Rolling On Throttle

Trail Braking (ease off brakes)

Exit

Apex

Turn In

Threshold Braking 100%

This shows how much braking and accelerating is done during each part of the racing line. A good sign of how well your kart is handling is how quickly you can apply full throttle. *Craig Ketchen*

eration. As you unwind the wheel you increase your radius, which in turn lets more grip to be applied to accelerating. Just like easing off the brakes coming in to a corner, you need to squeeze on the throttle as you go out of the corner and onto the straightaway. Depending on the two-cycle motor you have, you may find that after picking up the throttle you almost immediately go to full throttle. However, the mistake drivers make is thinking that you instantly go to full throttle. This is not the case. Momentum is key and you will usually begin to pick up the throttle somewhere before the apex to help settle the kart and keep up its cornering speed. Once again you will be flat on the gas and accelerating.

This may seem a little confusing at first. Imagine that you only ever have 100 percent of grip at any one time. It's all about a balance. Try to use that 100 percent of grip consistently throughout the corner, whether it is under braking, turning, or accelerating, or a combination of all the above.

THE RACING LINE
Sprint and Road Race

We know that sprint and road-race racetracks are made up of a mix of corners and straightaways. Usually the most time spent on a racetrack is on a straightaway at full throttle. Because of this, the goal is to be on full throttle the longest amount of time. Our objective is to make corners as straight and as fast as possible.

A racetrack will consist of four general types of corners: 90 degree, entry speed, exit speed, and combination corners.

The key to having fast corner speeds is to take the biggest radius possible through the corner. The basic formula is increased R= increased MPH, or the bigger the radius of the corner, the faster the miles per hour through the corner. It's simple when you think about it—this is the same reason you can go through a sweeper with a larger radius faster than a hairpin with a tight radius. To get the biggest radius in any corner means starting all the way wide on the entry, going all the way tight at the apex, then going all the way wide again on the exit. Each type of corner has various elements and details

to consider in order to demonstrate a perfect racing line.

A basic, or 90-degree, corner can be thought of as symmetrical. The radius is fairly constant through the turn, and the straightaway preceding the corner has about the same top speed as the straightaway following it. Based on what we know about the importance of straightaways, you can assess that both coming in fast (late braking) and exiting fast (acceleration) are equally important. Remember, to have the fastest corner speed, start by driving the largest radius possible. This means starting outside on the entry, going tight in the middle, and exiting again.

Remember that the brakes need to be applied properly. You want to squeeze the pedal, not stomp on it just because you're trying to brake very late. Applying brakes too aggressively

The key to having fast corner speeds is to take the biggest radius possible through the corner.

This is the racing line through a combination corner. Some drivers refer to these types of corner as "esses." *Craig Ketchen*

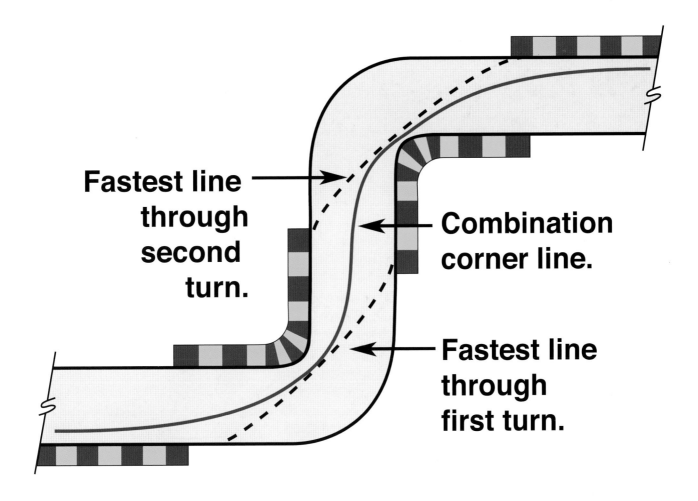

Fastest line through second turn.

Combination corner line.

Fastest line through first turn.

The best way to steer a kart that doesn't want to turn is with the throttle.

doesn't give the kart enough time to transfer weight. Be quick with your braking, but be smooth and efficient.

DRIVING TECHNIQUES

Indoor

The indoor driving technique is identical to the sprint track as far as specific line. The biggest difference that you will encounter on an indoor track is the normally slippery track conditions and the fact that you can't change or adjust the karts to suit these conditions. As we have discussed, slippery track conditions make the kart lay flat on the ground and generally produce an understeer due to the rear axle not picking up enough. If you try being patient and waiting for the kart to turn on its own, you will be giving up time.

The best way to steer a kart that doesn't want to turn is with the throttle. That means using the power of the motor to break the rear tires loose and slide the back of the kart, in turn steering the front. In many situations this happens in the middle of the turn. However, many times you will find this breaking away and steering the kart with the back end can happen as early just before your turn in.

It is a balance of breaking the back away with the throttle before turn in, balancing the slide with the brakes and speed at mid corner, then accelerating with minimal slide on the exit. This is a tricky technique that takes a lot of practice. The severity of this indoor technique depends on how slippery the track is or how pushy the kart is. The more sever the conditions, the more sever the slide technique.

The biggest mistake that most indoor drivers make is that they use the brakes to much to steer the kart, and not enough of the throttle. The disadvantage of strictly using the brakes is that by the time you hit the brakes to turn the kart, the

motor/clutch takes too much time to recover and the kart accelerates poorly. So, this slide technique is really a balance of the throttle and brakes working together.

Speedway

For Speedway racing, the line approach is much the same as the road course, but with a few key differences. The same idea for a fast line is that we are trying to slow down as little as possible while having the biggest radius we can. Just picture that an oval turn is only a longer version of the 90-degree road course corner that was talked about earlier.

You want to start wide on the turn in, get to an apex or tight line in the middle of the corner, and then exit wide again to make the radius as big as possible. The biggest differences that would change this basic line are track conditions, grip level, and/or specific track characteristics, like banking. For instance on a dirt oval, you will often find that where and when the track dries out after the initial track preparation may see the grippiest part of the track starting at the bottom and slowly moves up the racetrack as the day or night goes on. So, eventually, this may make a fast line that is nowhere close to the tightest or bottom part of the track. The only way to really find where this line lays is by experimenting during your sessions and watching other drivers.

On an asphalt oval, there generally aren't drastically changing track conditions like as on a dirt track. However, on both dirt and asphalt, tracks can be heavily banked. The way banking changes where the line may be because banking gives a kart more grip. If a track starts with minimal banking at the bottom, but increases in banking up the racetrack, the most grip may be somewhere in the middle where the maximum banking is. The other differ-

Banking changes where the line may be because banking gives a kart more grip.

ence on an oval track that may change the non-traditional line is what rpm your motor pulls best in. Most oval karts are non-shifters, usually geared for how long the straight is for maximum top speed. While the rpm in the turn is usually limited to how tight you line is, if you are driving a low and tight apex, you may find that your rpm drops below where the motor produces adequate torque. The tradeoff by driving the traditional tight apex and having the biggest radius still may not produce as much gain as moving your kart a little higher up the track and having the motor pull harder off the corner. The only way to know where to run on the track is to compare rpm, acceleration, and lap times of different lines you run in practice.

REFERENCE POINTS

"Hit your marks." You hear this all the time in racing. It's important because hitting the defined marks means you are driving the kart exactly where you think it needs to go. A technique that helps with this is to get used to looking for landmarks such as a pylon, a line on the track, a hay bale, a grease spot, or anything else that is clearly visible and can be used as a reference point. It's important that you get into the habit of looking around, opening your field of vision. (I actually look around both on and off the racetrack as much as possible when I drive.) Keep your eyes moving constantly, looking down the track, always in the direction where you want to go.

The reference points will come naturally. Looking around will help you be more consistent with your braking points, turn-in points, apex/release points, and acceleration points, lap after lap. Of course, it's always best to use reference points that can't be moved, like a fencepost or sign marker. Reference points can act as indicators of how you are progressing—especially for new drivers. As you begin to become more proficient in your kart, you'll find that your reference points may change. This is especially true for braking.

Some professional drivers view each section of a track as a page in a book. As you reach the exit point, you turn the page in your head and dig into the next section. This helps you to remain focused and "turn the page" on a bad section, making sure it doesn't affect the next section.

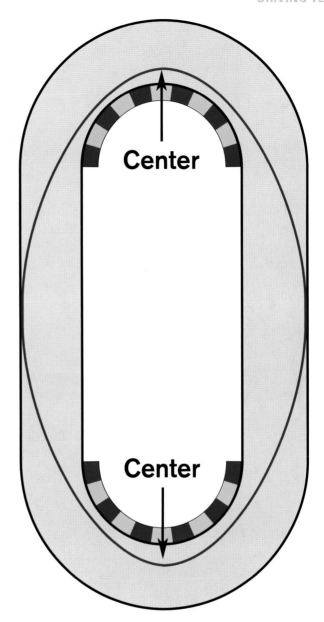

This is the proper speedway or oval racing line—shaped like a diamond. This racing line helps reduce the amount of tire scrub that occurs when the wheel is turning.
Craig Ketchen

When you arrive at the track, set up your pit area right away. This is a pit setup using the back of a pickup truck—the tailgate makes for a great bench. *Jeff Deskins*

Work out a schedule for the day so you know how much time you have and what you can do to get ready.

RACE-DAY SETUP: FAST OFF THE TRAILER

The most important part of racing is prepping your kart before you go to the track. The right preparation will not only help you win races, but will make racing much more enjoyable. Make sure you've checked every nut and bolt for tightness and make sure every drill bolt is properly cotter pinned or safety wired. As discussed, this exercise is great for uncovering any potential problems. Before you load up your gear, make sure your kart is race ready. I am a big believer in getting any work done on the kart *before* going to the track. That way, if there are any problems along the way, you won't have the added stress of still having to finish prepping your kart at the track.

Try to give yourself time to relax and prepare for the race. Work out a schedule for the day so you know how much time you have and what you can do to get ready. If possible, try not to work with your race suit on. Putting your suit on and getting ready to race should be a constant routine that helps you get focused and ready to win.

When you get to the track, get yourself set up and sign in immediately. Take a couple of minutes to scope out the area to find a good pit spot. (I always want to be central to the washrooms and the starting grid—during the race day you will spend a lot of time running between both of these places.) Unload your kart onto the kart stand and set up your pit area. A pop-up sunshade tent is

a great idea. Think about picking up a 12x12-foot (3.7x3.7-meter) piece of outdoor carpet at your local home-improvement store; it helps to keep the dirt and dust down in your pit area. Some tracks that pit on asphalt require a covering of some kind to keep spilled fuel or oil off the surface. Set up your tools on the tailgate of your truck or on a worktable. For karting, you don't need a lot of tools, so have them ready to go, laid out as you need them.

Organize all of your parts boxes so you can find them quickly and easily, and don't stack them 10 high so you spend your day sorting and searching for parts. Label the outside of each box

clearly or try to get different colored lids. Put all of your cleaners in one box, all your spare parts in another, etc. Try to find a pit layout that works for you and stick to it. You need to be able to find things quickly. Have all your charts ready on a clipboard so you can make notes. Fill in your primary chart indicating date, track, weather, event, class, and other details—see page 154 in the appendix for a race-day information sheet. Go to a general-purpose store and purchase a cigarette-lighter power adapter to run your computer. That way, if you get to a track and find they don't have a power outlet, you can run your computer off your car battery.

A typical pit setup using a large race trailer. When you need a little more pit space, folding tables can provide the space you need. *Sean Buur*

Have all your charts ready on a clipboard so you can make notes.

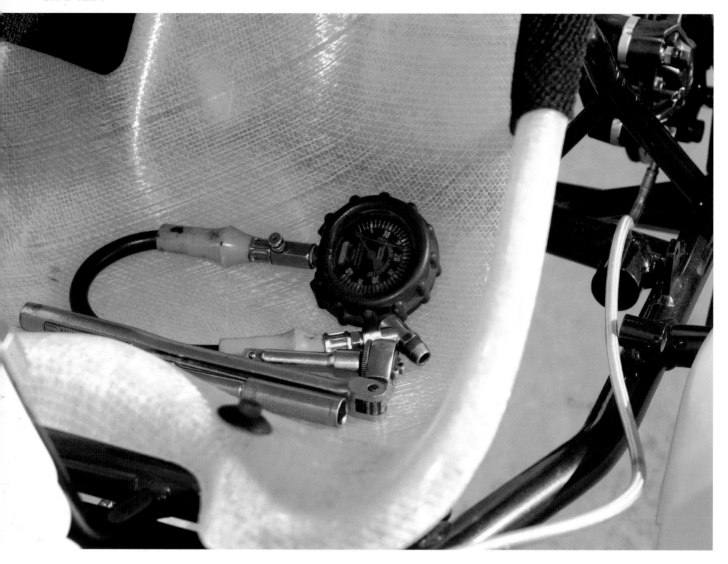

Check wheel nuts and air pressure before each track session. It is a good idea to place the necessary tools on your seat as a reminder. *Sean Buur*

Check all your fluid levels, including brake fluid and crankcase oil—this is also a good time to lube the chain.

Next, do a quick visual check of all fuel lines, fuel filters, and cables. Make sure fuel lines are not chaffing on anything. Check that you're getting full throttle. Remove the air filter and push on the throttle pedal. On butterfly-style carburetors the "butterfly" can actually go past vertical and start to close the venturi. Check that your throttle stops are set correctly to keep from stretching or breaking the cable. Make sure that the throttle cable slides inside the housing freely.

The next step is to write down your baseline chassis setup to make sure you can track your changes throughout the event. This will include settings like the front track width, rear track width, ride height, and tire pressures.

Set the tire pressures to your hot settings, then measure and write down the circumference of each tire. To keep the corner weights the same, it's usually best to have as close to equal tire circumferences as possible. However, if they are off, have the biggest rear tire on the side toward the outside of the track, and mount the bigger front tire on the side closest to the inside of the track. With the stagger set this way, the kart will turn better and scrub less speed for the majority of the corners on the track.

Make sure the front and rear hub bolts are tight, and check the wheel nuts on all four wheels. Check all your fluid levels, including brake fluid and crankcase oil—this is also a good time to

lube the chain. As we mentioned earlier, be deliberate and lube the chain from the inside out. When lubing the chain, more is not necessarily better. The idea is to apply only one coat of lube on the length of the chain. Applying any more than this will only create excess mess and attract more dust.

The next step is to warm up the engine. Add fuel and prime the fuel system, as previously discussed. Correctly priming the engine is the key to starting your kart on the first try, every time. It's easier to take the time to prime your fuel system correctly than to waste a lot of time and effort turning the kart engine over in the pits to fire off. You run the risk of killing the battery on your starter or breaking the recoil on the engine.

Be Prepared to Have Fun (And Win)

The last thing to do is locate a spot on the track to place your beacon (if you have one). The ideal spot is one that was used for practice sessions, that way data will overlay on top of itself with no differences. It's also very helpful to place the beacon in an area just before the pit in-road. This will keep you from doing an extra cool-down lap and save you time to use for making changes to your kart. Many times on a race weekend, the operator of the track will take the responsibility of placing a beacon. If it's more than a one-day event, don't count on the same beacon being out the entire weekend. For this reason, it's important that you know where the beacon is located in case you

When warming up a water-cooled engine, place your hand on the side of the cylinder to feel the temperature increase. If the temperature goes up really quickly, you may have a problem with the cooling system.
Jeff Deskins

MEMO'S SNACK TIP

A lot of drivers overlook the advantages to being well nourished at the racetrack. Part of the problem comes from the fact that preparing for the track usually requires things like working on the kart, mixing fuel, and loading the kart, which all take a fair amount of time. Packing snacks is usually the last thing on everybody's mind when heading out to drive. The other option is buying food at the snack stand at the track. Unfortunately, usually available are things like hot dogs, potato chips, and candy—none of which are great for good sustained energy.

My first favorite snack is PB&R sandwiches. It's a couple of slices of wheat bread with peanut butter and raisins. I also use the natural type of peanut butter, which contains no sugar. The result is a snack that has carbs, protein, and fruit all wrapped up in one. It's a snack for great instant energy, it keeps you going strong for the whole race, and it only takes a minute to make. Not to mention, PB&R sandwiches stand up to the harsh environment of the track better than any other good-for-you snack I know.

The other area that most drivers overlook is drinking enough liquids. On a hot day a driver will lose a few pounds of water in the way of sweat. If you don't replenish those liquids you will become dehydrated and fatigued. So, even before you take your first laps, drink up! I have tried numerous products over my driving years. So many of them are either too sweet, or have too much salt in them. My No. 1 favorite product to use is Cytomax sport drink by Cytosport products. It has the right amount of water, sodium, and electrolytes to let me perform at my best. I use Cytomax before, during, and after race days, and even during the hours I spend in the gym each day when not racing.

The first time out for the day, it's important to take the time to gradually warm up your engine and transmission.

have to replace it with your own. Make a note of the location of the beacon on your set-up sheet.

Now it's time to suit up and head out onto the track. Make sure all of your driving equipment is in good condition. Clean off your visor with a mild cleaner, using a clean paper towel to avoid scratches. Run your first set of practice laps. The first time out for the day, it's important to take the time to gradually warm up your engine and transmission. The first time out will also set the pattern for your procedures for the rest of the day. Get into the habit of doing certain things; at the end of your run, make sure you get used to coming off the track fast in order to get a good spark plug reading and tire pressure check.

Immediately, even before you take off your helmet, check your tire pressures and write them down—don't stand around talking with the other drivers. Lift your kart back onto the stand and head to your pit to keep from causing a lot of traffic at the scales. It's easier to remove any grease or grime while the kart is still warm, so once back at your pits, get out a rag and do a little cleaning. Download the data from your data acquisition system to your laptop computer. Make any notes as to how the kart handled on your set-up charts.

Keeping your energy level up is easily overlooked at the racetrack. You must take care of yourself as well as your kart. Don't forget to put some fuel in your body. Make sure you take in lots of fluids during the day. This should include things like water and pure juices, not soda or heavy drinks. Try to bring various types of fruit that you can snack on all day long—avoid the fast-food stand. Take some time between sessions to have a snack and to keep hydrated. A good time to do this is when the engine is cooling down before taking a plug reading.

As the engine cools, it's a good time to have a look around the kart and check for problem areas like chaffing hoses or loosening nuts and bolts. If your kart was prepared properly, rarely should something loosen or fall off. Pay close attention to the spindle bearing and brake/axle condition on a regular basis. Grab the front wheels and lift them up and down to check if the front spindles have any slop in them. Look at the rear rotor and make sure it's still centered, indicating that the axle hasn't moved. It's easy to lose a lot of time if the rotor is dragging on the brake pads.

Once the engine has cooled, do a plug check to give you an idea of how the carburetor jetting is set. Remember: after removing the spark plug put a piece of clean cloth in the plug hole; this will keep any dirt from getting into the combustion chamber. Plugging the hole will also keep cold air from rushing in and cooling the cylinder too quickly. For longer engine life, it is better that the piston and the cylinder cool down gradually.

After removing the plug, use the burn chart to decide whether or not to make a jet change. Even though jetting is not a critical factor with four-cycle engines, you should still get in the habit of checking the plug burn. By looking at it often enough and comparing it with how the engine is running, you will eventually start to see what a good-burning plug looks like. Also, you'll be able to see any possible wear or damage to the plug. Use a little anti-seize compound on the threads of your plug when you put it back in, to ensure that it will come out easily next time.

Finally, check for cracks in high-stress areas like your seat and engine mounts. Check the engine-mount bolts, chain tension, and wheel nuts. After lubing the chain, you should be ready to go out for your next session.

RACING PRINCIPLES

At this point we've done everything we can to prepare for race day. The kart is ready, the engine is tweaked, the gear is all set, and you're ready to go racing. Now it's time to put your helmet on and climb inside your kart to prepare for what you can expect while out on the track. Obviously you can't be prepared for every situation you will encounter, but there are a number of things to think about.

Practice

Proper practice procedure is critical to having a successful weekend. Your kart should always be ready to go as soon as you get to the track. A guaranteed way to lose valuable practice time is to still be working on your kart while others are out on the track fine-tuning theirs. The only things that you should have to do when you arrive at the track are the necessities such as checking wheel nuts, air and fuel in the kart, plugging in your

computer, and warming up the engine—that's it. Also, get your kart on the track scales as soon as possible to make sure it's at weight before starting to make any changes to the setup.

If it's a new track, walk the track and look for subtleties such as banking or surface changes that are hard to notice with just driving. Also, write out a game plan for things you want to try during the practice day. This helps you keep focused, while making sure that you have all the parts and tools to carry out your plan. Some people like to sit out sessions to allow the track to gain grip before they start putting wear on their equipment. This works if it's your home track and you have the experience to really know how the track will change. However, on most tracks, it's valuable to get a sense of the early conditions so that you have a better idea of how the track might continue to change throughout the weekend.

Once you hit the track, the number-one mistake most new drivers make is that they just drive around and don't really pay attention. On a new track, it is important to learn the track in the shortest time possible. Remembering land markers will help you with things like braking points, turn-in points, etc. This will help to get you up to speed quickly. After a few laps of learning the track, start to think about how the kart is handling; keep it simple at first. Is the kart understeering, oversteering, or is the traction poor?

Qualifying

One of the most important things to find out before a race is the qualifying procedure. Is it a two-lapper, five-lapper, or possibly a qualifying session where you can take as many runs as you like during the allotted time? Finding out the procedure is important so you

Pay close attention to the spindle bearing and brake/axle condition on a regular basis.

Check for cracks in high-stress areas like your seat and engine mounts.

Walk the track and look for subtleties such as banking or surface changes that are hard to notice with just driving.

Changes like more caster, positive camber, or moving your weight up will all possibly allow the kart to transfer more weight and load the tires harder in order to come in faster.

can tune your kart and better prepare yourself for a good run.

Many clubs/tracks use a green/white/checkered procedure for qualifying. This is the two-lap run, and your best time is taken for the grid. On a short session like this, you may never really be able to get your tires up to an ideal temperature, like you would during practice. For this session, you might want to make changes to your kart, helping it come in faster. Changes like more caster, positive camber, or moving your weight up will all possibly allow the kart to transfer more weight and load the tires harder in order to come in faster. You might also consider bumping up your tire pressures a couple of pounds for the short run. You can find out exactly how much by simulating a two-lap run during practice to see how the pressures come in.

Once on the track, it's important that you get up to speed as quickly as possible, without being overly sideways on the warm-up lap. Drive the warm-up lap as fast as you can. With the hard compound tires that most classes run, the tires will almost certainly have more grip on the second lap. On a two-lap run, you don't have the luxury of trying again. For that reason, it's critical that you work on this short qualifying in practice so you learn to get the most out of your kart in a short period of time without making a big mistake.

Also common is the five-lap run with multiple karts on the track with you. The starter usually tries to separate the drivers going out so that they get laps without traffic. Once the starter lets you out, look around the track to see where the other drivers are. Take that warm-up lap to try to position yourself by either slowing down or speeding up to get a gap. On a five-lap run, your tires will have a chance to get up to good operating temperatures, but you still may start them at a little higher psi than

for a race. On a five-lap run, try to get a solid lap in, then drive a little beyond the edge to try to get that one fast lap.

The last type of qualifying session is usually a group session that lasts between 15 and 30 minutes. Generally, they limit the group to around 15 drivers and you are allowed to come in and out of the pits as often as you want. The key to this type of session is to try to time your lap when you have no traffic and when the track is at its fastest. It's also important that you do as few laps as possible on your tires because you usually have to race on the same tires; try to limit the laps to under 10 total. The softer the tire compound, the fewer laps you want to do.

Starting

Starting from the front also has its own pressures and problems for the driver. After qualifying up front, the race is basically yours to lose. You have the best position for winning, but that certainly doesn't guarantee a win. It's great to be happy about qualifying up front, but just like in any position, don't dwell on qualifying times or position. Rather, start thinking about how you are going to win the race. This is where all those practice notes start to pay off. How was your kart on long runs? What are some of the changes that you may want to make to speed up your kart? What are you going to do for gearing? Remember, being at the front means that you won't be getting much of a draft from other karts. In this case, make sure to have good pull off the corners and max out your rpm down the straights.

It's important that you think about when and where you want your kart handling at its best. If you're in front, you definitely want to have great handling on the corner that leads to the straight with the most passing. If you are strong there, other drivers won't ever get the chance to be close enough to pass you. Every driver at one time has had a fast kart in the beginning, only to see the handling decrease as they slowly get shuffled to the back. Generally speaking, you want your kart to be at its best during the last half of the race.

People say you can't win the race on the first corner. Although this is true, the race isn't won until the checkered flag falls; you can surely pass or be passed by a lot of drivers. People mistake this advice for meaning that you should just sit back and not be aggressive—I totally disagree. The start of the race is when you see the most excitement, and you *must* be the most aggressive. The bottom line is that you can't allow yourself to be pushed around; you have to be on the defensive *and* offensive at all times.

The first key to a good start is watching the flagman and studying his actions on previous race starts. Does he flinch just before he waves the green? Does he throw them early or late? (When I raced KT100 locally, we had one flagger who always moved his knee just before he threw the flag. When he did this, I always knew to stand on the gas and go.)

Passing

No matter where you start, after you take the green flag you will no doubt be trying to pass or be defending from being passed. The key to both situations is to be relaxed and not lose your concentration. The easiest place to pass is down the straightaway and under braking. The key to doing this successfully is to set it up from the corner before.

If you remember from the basic line theory, increased R=increased MPH, we want to maximize the speed through the last turn before the pass. The mistake that most drivers make is that they get too anxious coming off the

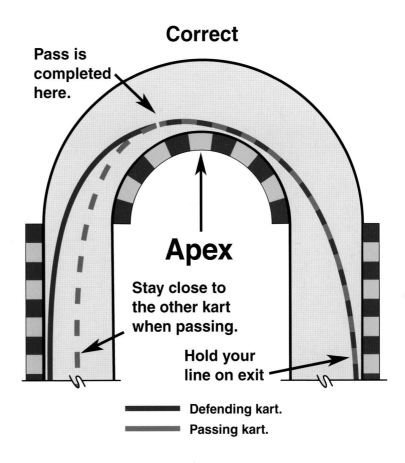

Correct

Pass is completed here.

Apex

Stay close to the other kart when passing.

Hold your line on exit

▬▬▬ Defending kart.
▬▬▬ Passing kart.

turn by pulling out early and scrubbing their speed. The key is to leave a little gap so you can still take the ideal line through the corner. Hopefully, as you exit the corner slightly faster, you will be able to close the gap and eventually pick up the other driver's draft to help slingshot you past. Another mistake drivers make when they pass is they then overcharge the next turn and lose the position. The idea when making a pass is that you just need to control the other driver's line to guarantee that you will complete the pass.

All you want to do is get alongside the driver. As long as you are on the inside, the other driver will have no choice but to wait for you to turn into the corner. Once you turn into the corner, you will intercept the ideal line and control the other driver's acceleration on the exit.

If you are the one being passed,

This is the proper racing line for passing. Position your kart alongside the kart you are passing to ensure they cannot move to block your pass. *Craig Ketchen*

The start of the race is when you see the most excitement, and you must be the most aggressive.

Memo Gidley makes the inside pass on co-author Jeff Grist at Moran Raceway in Beaumont, California.
Sean Buur

don't give up the position easily. If possible, you may find that if you make the other driver really work for the position, they might make a mistake that will help you keep the position. And even if they do pull off a clean pass, immediately try to set them up for your own pass. This is especially important if you know that they are faster and will be able to pull away if you don't counterattack right away. Also, be aware of other drivers behind both of you. If you fight for the position too hard you'll both go slower. Doing this too much may allow another group of drivers to catch up. Sometimes it's best to work with the driver in front to try to break away from the rest of the field. This is done by not attempting to pass the driver in front, which should give him the

idea that you want to do some drafting.

Drafting a driver in front does not mean putting pressure on them in the turns. If you pressure the driver in front of you in the corners, they will more than likely start to make mistakes, slowing both of you down. The best way is to leave them space on the corners. The area that you really make up the time in drafting together is down the straight. In a perfect world, the best way to draft is to literally push the driver in front of you down the straightway. However, most tracks forbid actually making contact with the driver in front. So you want to get as close to the driver in front as possible. This way, the driver in front is using his motor to punch a hole in the air, and you are using your kart to close the hole. You both have less drag than if you were doing it all by yourself and you will go faster. If you are the driver in back, you may find that you must back off the gas to keep from making contact with the driver in front. When you feel like you have a comfortable gap on the drivers behind you, then you can start to try to make the pass for position.

Defense

Defending from a pass is also a critical part of a successful race. Even if you started at the front, you may find another driver who has a better setup for the beginning of the race. Getting passed early on will make it that much harder to get back to the front at the end of the race. The most obvious form of defense is blatant blocking [glossary]—weaving down the straight to block the other driver's momentum, making him lay off the gas. This, however, is not recommended, as it upsets the driver behind, forcing him to make a drastic pass, which has a good chance of taking you both out of the race. The other way to keep from getting passed is to take an extremely tight line going into the corners. The problem with this is that it's not a very good offense. Driving an extremely tight line will slow your corner speed, which will allow the driver behind to get a run on you and attempt to pass.

The best defense is to make it just a little harder for the driver behind to get by. You can turn into the corner slightly early and drive down the straight a couple of feet to the inside. Both of these make it a little harder for the driver behind to get by while not having a big effect on your speed. The other key is to never over charge the corner to keep the driver behind. Whatever you do, it's important to slow down your kart with enough control that you can get on the gas early and be fast coming

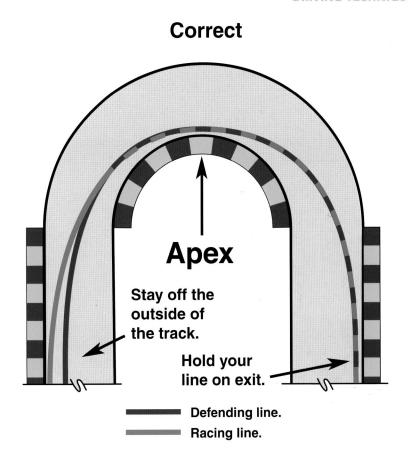

Correct

Apex

Stay off the outside of the track.

Hold your line on exit.

▬▬▬ Defending line.
▬▬▬ Racing line.

off the corner. This makes it harder for a driver to get a run on you going into the next straightaway.

Dealing with traffic is another area where being aggressive and committed is key. If you are going to make a pass, commit to it. The reason most accidents occur is because a driver just sticks a nose in or doesn't really get his kart all the way in. If you try to pass a lapper and it looks like you can't make it happen, pull back and try again on the next corner. Most slower drivers you will pass usually have no idea you're coming up on them. It's important that you waste as little time as possible getting by in order to keep other drivers from catching up.

Finish First

Have you heard of the saying, "to finish first you must first finish?" The ultimate goal is to be fast and finish the race. Just to be one and not the other is not anyone's idea of satisfying. Most

This is the proper line to defend your position in a corner. Place your kart low going into the corner to keep the driver behind you, while still being able to make the corner.
Craig Ketchen

Never over charge the corner

to keep the driver behind.

Stay with your kart until you are absolutely sure that you have been released from tech.

Not every race day goes according to plan. Here Rob Howden, editor of *Super Kart Illustrated Magazine* and renowned race announcer, parks his kart into the hay bails during the 2005 Rock Island Grand Prix. *Sean Buur*

of finishing the race really comes down to preparation of your kart and yourself. Take the time to make sure your kart is in as good a condition as it can be. Make sure your body is also physically able to go the race distance. When you get tired, your concentration is the first to go. If you can prepare yourself in those two areas, then it will just come down to getting yourself and your kart fast. This is all about practice and being smart. If you use your time better and smarter than your competitors, you have a better chance at being faster than them. Take notes. There is no easier way to track progress and get faster than keeping a comprehensive notebook.

Postrace Etiquette

If you do well, you may be called into a tech area. It's important that you understand what is and what is not allowed in the tech area—drivers have been

disqualified after a good race because a friend comes up to them in the tech area. Make sure you stay with your kart until you are absolutely sure that you have been released from tech. Remember, many club races are run with rotating volunteers who help with tech. Make sure you talk to the person in charge.

Everybody celebrates a win and a loss in different ways. The most important thing about a race weekend is learning from your mistakes. Whether you've won or lost, there are always things you might have done better. Make notes and comments on these while they are still fresh in your mind. If you can come back the next weekend better prepared, you will have a better chance of winning.

Drive-Home Kart Preparation

Before I load up to go home, I make mental notes of areas that I can improve on for the next time out. These may range

The end of race day can be a great time to talk about the days track events. Karting offers the opportunity to create memories that will last a lifetime. *Sean Buur*

from kart preparation, to ideas learned from handling, to the simplest of things like a pit spot. However, it's important that you go over these improvements while they are still fresh in your mind. Take the time to make all of your final notes and complete all of the charts. File these by track and event so you can go back to them the next time out.

Be sure to drain and replace the crankcase oil. As mentioned earlier, let the oil flow over your fingers and look for any contaminants. Be sure to replace the oil immediately and replace the filler cap. Don't dispose of used oil in an unsafe manner. Most tracks have a used-oil drum.

Before transporting your kart, do a couple of basic things. Drain all the fuel out of the fuel tank and carburetor. It's much easier on the fuel system to not be submersed in fuel for the week or so until you go out again. Take the time to wipe the grease off your kart while it's still fresh. This will also give you a chance to visually check for any parts that may have broken and need replacing.

WET WEATHER: THE GREAT EQUALIZER

Rain has been called the great equalizer, and for good reason. Racing in the rain reduces the influence of big horsepower and the latest features of the newest chassis. What becomes important is how well you set up your kart and drive it in extremely slippery conditions. Racing in wet weather is done in most sprint and road-race applications. Speedway racing is never in the wet, especially in dirt oval karting. Be sure to check with your local club to see if they race in the rain and what the specified tire is for those conditions. Most local clubs will call the race a wet-weather race and all drivers are

Wet conditions make it very difficult to get the kind of inside rear wheel lift that you need to turn the corner.

The dry weather racing line and the wet weather racing line are different. When it's wet, keep away from the surface of the track that has a lot of rubber. *Craig Ketchen*

required to run on wet weather tires. This is done for the safety of the drivers to avoid the problems that can occur if a kart doesn't have rain tires

Another big factor with rain set up is that the conditions always change. As people in the Midwest like to say, "If you don't like the weather, just wait 10 minutes." The track may go from being wet with the sun out, to quickly drying in patches in just a few laps. How much you change your chassis setup or driving style will depend on how quickly the weather is changing, for better or worse. If you want to get an unfair advantage in the rain, just be

prepared. Most racers don't spend enough time preparing for foul weather. There are a number of unique components and specific changes that need to be made to your kart to race in the rain.

How Rain Changes Everything

Because of the low-grip conditions created by the rain, you will never generate the amount of side force normally found in dry conditions, and major changes need to be made to the chassis setup. What is usually encountered in the rain is extreme understeer. This is because wet conditions make it very difficult to get the kind of inside

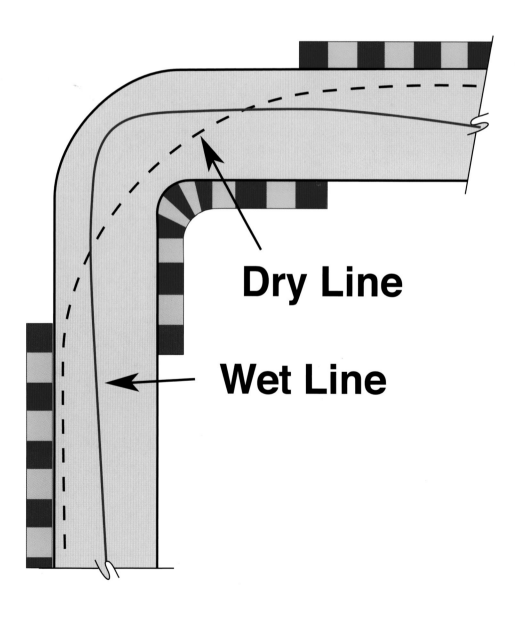

Dry Line

Wet Line

rear wheel lift that you need to turn the corner. As we said earlier, not getting the right amount of rear-wheel lift causes the front end to push.

The other area that can change in wet weather is driving technique. When it's dry, you drive your ideal line, based on the theory of increased R=increased MPH. With more or less everybody driving the same line, eventually the track builds up grip as the rubber is laid down. The problem is that the same rubber that helps with grip in the dry actually hurts grip in the wet.

The reason for this is simple, built-up rubber does not allow the water to soak into the track. It has the same effect as laying a tarp flat on the ground and soaking it with water—the tarp would be extremely slippery to walk on because the water has no place to go. The other reason is that excess oils like chain lube, fuel, and transmission oil collect on the racing line. Everyone knows the effects of trying to mix oil

and water: it's impossible. On the track, the combination of oil and water makes for an extremely slippery racing line.

By now you should have a good understanding of the dry racing-line theories previously discussed. Have you ever heard somebody say, "In the wet, stay off the racing line?" As mentioned earlier, the combination of rubber buildup and oils collected on the track make for an extremely slippery racing line. Because of these slick conditions, the racing line has to be modified in order to get the most grip for braking, turning, and accelerating. How is this done?

The easiest way to think about this is in wet conditions, drive the track in a completely opposite line from wherever you drive in dry conditions. As extreme as it may sound, this is really a good place to start. If you brake on the left side of the track when it's dry, brake on the right when it's wet. If you apex on the inside of the turn in dry conditions, try to apex on the outside of the turn in

Rain tires have deep grooves and very distinct patterns. The grooves pull water away from the surface to ensure the best grip. This is a rain tire from Bridgestone Racing, and has the pattern and shape molded into the tread. *Sean Buur*

The same rubber that helps with grip in the dry actually hurts grip in the wet.

When racing in the rain, drivers need to be very aggressive while turning the kart to ensure the inside rear wheel lifts off the ground. Finding enough grip is always a challenge when racing in wet conditions. *Todd McCall*

wet ones. If you exit on the outside, try exiting on the inside. In effect, what you are doing is crisscrossing the racing line.

How much you avoid the dry racing line really depends on how slippery that line is in the wet. If it's not too slick, you just need to change your line a little. If it's extremely slick, you need to change your line a lot.

Preparation

You will find that many of the components you use for wet conditions do not apply in dry conditions. For this reason, have one box or area where the entire rain setup is stored. In the case of a sudden rain shower, having everything in one spot will make the changeover to a rain setup much easier and quicker.

Also, watch the weather. In the old days, before weather radar, the Ferrari F1 team would call all the Italian restaurants in the area to see where the weather was

and if it was raining or not. This trick helped to keep Ferrari on top of their game. Weather tracking has become far more advanced these days. It can be as easy as watching the local newscasts.

What you pick up from doing this will help you forecast your own race-day weather. If you have access to the Internet, you can also get live satellite feeds that show precipitation levels in your area. On race day you could also have a radio tuned to the local weather channel.

Rain tires, as you might imagine, are very different from slicks. Most noticeably, they are made with grooves that are designed to push the water out and away from the tire. For maximum grip, rains are also made from a very soft compound rubber. You would think that this soft rubber would wear out quickly, but in wet conditions, the soft rubber lasts longer because the water on the track cools the rain tires. However, when rain tires do overheat because of drying track conditions, they begin to chunk and will fall apart quite easily.

There are a number of things you can do to your kart to have a trouble-free day in the rain. The first area to take care of is the air filter. Rain tires kick up a fine mist of water and grit from the track surface. If this is sucked into the carburetor, the engine will misfire. Suck enough water into the engine and you're looking at a possible piston seizure or, at the very least, excessive engine wear.

To protect your engine from the elements, you need to replace your high-flow gauze-style air filter with an air box and rain hood of some kind. To date, no one manufactures a rain system for four-cycle karts. Racers have used everything from pop bolts to Big Gulp cups to keep water out of their engines. The rain hood needs to be positioned

so the mist won't get in. This usually means facing backward, toward an area of clean air. Because of the extra weight of the air box and/or rain hood, it's important to use a mounting bracket to secure it. Supporting the air box will stop it from bouncing excessively and coming off the carburetor. It's important that you constantly clean the air filter and/or air box in between sessions to keep them from plugging up.

Wet weather will also pose some potential problems for your electronics, since water conducts electricity. Having your electronics in an area that gets wet may allow the water to short out the electrical system. If this happens, you are bound to get a misfire.

The best solution is to have all your electronics mounted in a dry place. Various-sized electronics boxes can be purchased at an electronics store; they

To protect your engine from the elements, you need to replace your high-flow gauze-style air filter with an air box and rain hood of some kind.

Wet weather racing can mean messy track conditions. The driver and kart need to be well prepared to deal with the poor conditions this type of racing can experience. Be sure to clean your gear and your kart right after the race. *Sean Buur*

Buy a two-piece suit so you have the option of just wearing the top or bottom if conditions begin to dry.

Try to avoid standing water or puddles on the track. An excessive amount of water can flood the engine and end your race. Most races will not run if too much water accumulates on the track surface. *Sean Buur*

will house your ignition box, sealing it watertight. Keep the coil dry and seal up any areas susceptible to water seepage, such as where the spark lead is attached. Make sure you have a good watertight spark-plug boot.

For the data-acquisition system, similar steps should be taken to prevent potential problems caused by wet weather. The most fragile components are the dash and the logging unit. The dash is very susceptible to water because it's located on the steering wheel, which places it in the path of water and rain. I've found that you can take a clear sandwich bag and tye wrap it over the dash. It keeps the water out, yet the numbers are still visible.

The logging unit is somewhat better protected from the elements due to its location under the front fairing. However, shielding it from any water

that may get splashed on it will help to keep it protected. Again, using a plastic bag is a great way to seal it from water.

Driver

There is no quicker way to spoil a perfectly good day of driving in the rain than being cold and wet. Aside from making you uncomfortable, getting cold will have the effect of tightening your muscles, which will slow your reflexes and reaction times. To be fast in the rain you have to have lightning-quick reflexes.

A good rain suit is a worthwhile investment. You want something that is fully water repellent, but not so heavy that it restricts your movement. Buy a two-piece suit so you have the option of just wearing the top or bottom if conditions begin to dry. If you're heading to the track and forget your rain suit, most general-merchandise stores carry rain suits that

will get you by for the day. Also, having an extra change of socks, T-shirt, and underwear to keep you warm and dry will come in handy in wet conditions.

Hands and feet are a little harder to keep dry. You can buy slip-on rubber coverings that do a good job of keeping your feet dry. However, they are definitely a little cumbersome. The other solution is to have an extra pair of driving shoes and always start with a dry pair. You can also purchase a boot dryer from a local shoe store. These units do an excellent job of drying your shoes between sessions.

As far as keeping your hands dry, nothing does a great job at keeping water out. You can purchase watercraft or wetsuit gloves that, although not waterproof, do keep wet hands warm. The only drawback to these types of gloves is that they are not abrasion resistant, a requirement for karting safety.

I think the best plan of attack is to have a couple of pairs of gloves with you at the track and to dry them in between sessions. If you don't have a heater, start your car and use the dash heater to dry your gloves. Kart races are usually short enough that if you start with a pair of warm and dry gloves, your hands will stay warm until the end of the race.

Helmet preparation is very important to your visibility on the track. If you can't see, you're not going to be able to drive very well. The first area on a helmet that needs to be addressed is the air vents. Any water that makes its way into the helmet through these vents will fog your visor. Vents on the top or sides of the helmet should be taped to prevent water from working its way inside.

As far as the shield itself, many helmet manufacturers make an anti-fog visor that's designed with a special coating or layer that prevents fogging. These usually do a great job, as long as the shield is relatively new. Special care should be taken when cleaning this style of visor, as it's easy to scratch or rub off the fog coating. Also, you can buy a number of different anti-fog solutions or coatings that you can apply to your existing shield. These are available from racing performance shops or your local ski shop.

Make sure your shield seals around the helmet to prevent water seepage. This is accomplished with the foam or rubber liner that runs around the outside of the eye port. If this is torn or missing, it would be a good idea to replace it. You can usually purchase new liner strips from your helmet manufacturer.

Vents on the top or sides of the helmet should be taped to prevent water from working its way inside.

While drivers need to be aggressive turning into the corner, you still need to be very smooth around the track. This is especially important when braking or accelerating in order to avoid the wheels locking up or spinning. *Sean Buur*

Glossary

KARTING SPEAK

ACKERMANN STEERING a geometric arrangement of linkages in the steering of a kart or other vehicle designed to solve the problem of wheels on the inside and outside of a turn needing to trace out circles of different radii.

AIR DENSITY the mass per volume of Earth's atmosphere; a useful value in engine performance tuning.

BAFFLE a flat plate that controls or directs the flow of fluid or energy

BALANCING to bring into or maintain in a state of equilibrium

BALLAST any heavy material used to add weight to the kart

BLOCKING to obstruct the movement of an opponent

BLUEPRINTING matching an engine's specifications to the original blueprint designs used to create the engine molds, removing any manufacturing defects or tolerances from the existing parts

BORED to make a hole in or through, with or as if with a drill or specialized machine

CAMBER the relationship of a vehicle's front or rear wheels as it relates to the bottom and the top

CARBURETION to combine or mix (a gas, for example) with volatile hydrocarbons, so as to increase available fuel energy.

CASTER the rearward facing angle on a wheel axle used to create stability in the wheel.

CENTER OF GRAVITY the point in or near a body at which the gravitational potential energy of the body is equal to that of a single particle of the same mass located at that point and through which the resultant of the gravitational forces on the component particles of the body acts

CHASSIS FLEX the physical bending or twisting of the kart chassis to permit the transfer of weight, generally occurring as the vehicle changes direction or velocity.

CLUTCH any various device for engaging and disengaging two working parts of a shaft or of a shaft and a driving mechanism

CLUTCH LOCK-UP when a clutch is fully engaged and transferring 100 percent of the power from the engine to the drivetrain

CONTACT PATCH the part of the tire that touches the track surface
Controlled slip: setting a clutch to allow a certain amount of slip that will engage the power slowly

DETONATION the result of preignition

DIFFERENTIAL a bevel gear that permits rotation of two shafts at different speeds; used on the rear axle of automobiles to allow wheels to rotate at different speeds on curves

DIFFUSER a device, such as a cone or baffle

DOUBLE NUTTING using two nuts on the same end of the same bolt that are locked together to ensure the component being bolted into place does not come loose.

DRAFTING to move, ride, or drive close behind a fast-moving object so as to take advantage of the slipstream, especially in a race

ELECTRODES a solid electric conductor through which an electric current enters or leaves an electrolytic cell or other medium

ENDPLAY the movement built into components of a clutch to allow them to spin freely without creating friction.

FINGER TIGHT to tighten by hand and not with a wrench or mechanical device.

FLASH POINT the lowest temperature at which the vapor of a combustible will ignite in air

FLATHEAD the physical shape of a Briggs & Stratton side-valve engine produced from the early 1950s to the late 1980s.

FOUR-STROKE an internal combustion engine with four up-and-down piston actions to complete the power stroke

FREEWHEEL a power-transmission device that allows the drive shaft of a motor vehicle to continue turning when its speed is greater than that of the engine shaft

GRIP the friction between a body and the surface on which it moves—as between an a kart tire and the road

HONING done to finish the surface of an engine cylinder so it matches the size of the piston and ring being installed

HOPPING to move over by hopping.

JETTING adjusting the flow of fuel and air into an internal combustion engine using the internal jets

LIFT the distance which something is raised or rises

LOADING UP a two-cycle engine that receives too much fuel from the carburetor

METHANOL a colorless, toxic, flammable liquid used as an antifreeze, a general solvent, and fuel

NEGATIVE CAMBER a setting of wheels in which they are further apart at the bottom than at the top.

OVERSTEER to turn more sharply than the operator would expect

PLAY to move or operate freely within a bounded space

PLUMB in a vertical or perpendicular line

POSITIVE CAMBER a setting of wheels in which they are closer together at the bottom than at the top.

PRE-IGNITION the ignition of fuel in an internal-combustion engine before the spark passes through the fuel, resulting from a hot spot in the cylinder or from too great a compression ratio for the fuel

PUSH when the front end of the kart does not turn properly because of a lack of front end grip when cornering

RANGE the maximum extent or distance limiting operation, action, or effectiveness

REV LIMITER an electronic device used on an internal combustion engine to limit the maximum allowable crankshaft revolutions to a preset number.

RICH a fuel mixture with a larger proportion of fuel than air

ROLLING RESISTANCE the resistance experienced as a kart rolls along the track surface

SCALING to weigh with scales

SCRUBBING the dragging of race tires against the track surface as the vehicle changes direction

SEATING to fix firmly in place

SLICKS a racing tire with a smooth tread.

SLOSH an uneven or unsecured movement of the driver in a kart seat

STALL SPEED This is set rpm level at which the clutch hits the engagement point, that is the clutch is fully locked and is transferring 100% of the power to the drive train.

STOPS a part in a mechanism that stops or regulates movement

TOE ANGLE the relationship of a vehicle's front or rear wheels as it relates to the front edge and the back edge

TORQUE a force that produces rotation or torsion

TWO-STROKE an internal combustion engine with two up-and-down piston actions to complete the power stroke

UNDERSTEER to turn less sharply than the operator would expect

VENTURI a constricted throat in the air passage of a carburetor, causing a reduction in pressure that results in fuel vapor being drawn out of the carburetor bowl

VERTICAL upright in position

WANDERING to proceed in an irregular course

WEIGHT BALANCE the action of scaling a kart to ensure it meets minimum required weight and that the weight is distributed in the desired percentages

WEIGHT TRANSFER the movement of weight from one side of the chassis to the other as the vehicle changes direction or velocity

Basic Nut and Bolt Check List*

Date: _____   Kart: _____   Mechanic: _____

✓	Safety Wire	Cotter Pin	Other	Notes
Front End				
King Pin Bolts		YES		
Master Cylinder	YES			
Tie Rod Heim Jam Nuts			Left & Right Thread	Tight
Tie Rod End Bolts		YES		
Steering Support Bracket		YES		
Steering Wheel	YES			
Front Spindles			Safety Clip	Castellated Nut
Steering Wheel Hub		YES		
Engine				
Ignition and Coil				Snug
Pipe and Silencer			Springs	Cradle
Motor Mount Bolts			Thread Lock	
Carburetor Mounting Bracket			Clamp	Tight
Fuel Pump			Bushing	Snug
Cooling System				
Mounting Brackets			Bushings	Tight
Hose Fittings			Hose Clamps	Tight
Rear End				
Bearing Cassettes (if adjustable)			Thread Lock	Snug
Bearing Set Screws			Thread Lock	Tight
Axle Collars			Clean Surface	Tight
Rear Hubs			Clean Surface	Tight
Rear Brake Caliper	YES			
Rear Brake Rotor Bolts	YES			
Body Work and Bumpers				
Front Bumper				Snug
Rear Bumper			Nylock Nut	Snug
Front Faring Top and Bottom			Rubber Bushings	Snug
Nerf Bar			Nylock Nut	Snug
Side Pods			Nylock Nut	Snug
Floor Pan			Nylock Nut	Snug
Fuel Tank				Snug
Seat				
Right and Left Side Supports			Nylock Nut	Tight
Seat Struts Top Bolt			Nylock Nut	As Required
Seat Strut Bottom Bolt			Nylock Nut	Tight
Front Mounting Tabs			Nylock Nut	Tight

*Example only. Consult your dealer for a detailed maintenance program.

Reproduced with permission from Secrets of Speed Publications, Inc. copyright 2005

Quick Maintenance Chart*

Date: _____ Kart: _____ Mechanic: _____

	Pre-Race	After Each Session	After Each Event	Once a month
Front End	Clean	Check	Clean	Re-assemble
Brake/Rotor/Caliper	Clean	Check Fluid	Replace Fluid	Check Pads
Front Hubs or Spindles	Check Bearings	Adjust	Clean	Re-assemble
Alignment	Check			Adjust
Engine	Remove and Clean	Check	Replace Oil	Top End Rebuild
Ignition and Coil	Check	Check	Inspect	Re-assemble
Pipe and Silencer	Inspect	Check	Clean	Re-assemble
Carburetor	Clean	Adjust	Clean	Inspect
Chain	Adjust	Lube	Inspect	Replace
Cooling System	Check Clamps	Check Level	Inspect	Replace Fluid
Rear Axle	Clean and Inspect	Clean	Remove	Inspect
Bearing and Cassettes	Clean	Check	Clean	Inspect
Set Screws/Axle Collars	Check	Check	Check	Check
Rear Hubs	Clean	Check	Check	Clean
Body Work and Bumpers	Clean	Inspect	Clean	Re-assemble
Seat	Clean	Inspect	Clean	Re-assemble

Glossary:

Clean – Follow the cleaning instructions to remove all grease grime and grit from the surface.
Check – Quick check to ensure level or tightness on tension is correct.
Inspect – Do a visual and physical inspection for damage, cracks and wear.
Adjust – Make regular adjustments as required
Re-assemble – Take the component apart, clean and re-assemble.
Replace – Remove old part and replace with a new part.

Scaling Chart

Date: _____ Kart: _____ Driver: _____

Location: _____ Engine: _____ Class Weight: _____

Tire: _____ Wheel: _____ Other: _____

Left	Front	Right
_____ %	_____ %	_____ %
_____ lbs/kg	_____ lbs/kg	_____ lbs/kg

Caster: _____   Caster: _____

Toe: _____   Toe: _____

Run Out: _____   Run Out: _____

PSI: _____   PSI: _____

Front Track

Rear Track

Draw in placement of lead.

Run Out: _____   Run Out: _____

PSI: _____   PSI: _____

_____ %   _____ %

_____ lbs/kg   _____ lbs/kg

_____ lbs/kg

_____ %

Rear

_____ %   _____ %

_____ lbs/kg   _____   _____ lbs/kg

Total   Total   Total

Notes: _____

_____

_____

_____

Baseline Set-up

Date: _____ Kart: _____ Driver: _____

Location: _____ Engine: _____ Class Weight: _____

Tire: _____ Wheel: _____ Other: _____

Spindle: _____   Front Track   Spindle: _____

Camber: _____   Camber: _____

Caster: _____   Caster: _____

Toe: _____   Toe: _____

Run Out: _____   Run Out: _____

PSI: _____   PSI: _____

Run Out: _____   Run Out: _____

PSI: _____   PSI: _____

Offset: _____   Offset: _____

Height: _____   Height: _____

Rear Track

Axel

Hubs: _____   Torsion Bar: _____   4th Rail: _____

Front Gear: _____   Rear Gear: _____   Ratio: _____

Notes: _____

_____

_____

_____

Pre-Race Tuning Checklist

Track: _____   Date: _____ By: _____

Time	Temp.	Humidity	Barometer	Oxygen	Ignition	Jet Size

Race Day Set-up

Date: _____ Track: _____ Event: _____

Class: _____ Kart: _____ Engine: _____

Session: _____

Hot: Cold: Front Track   Cold: Hot:

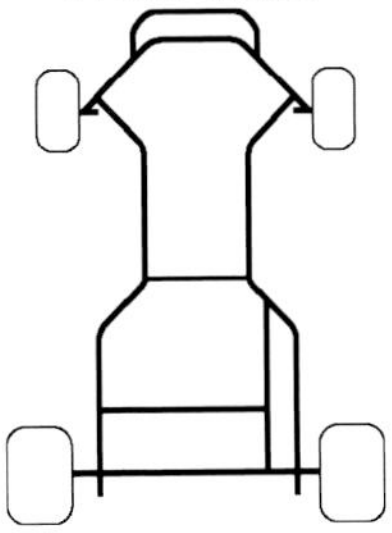

_____   _____   _____   _____

_____   _____   _____   _____

Rear Track

Notes: _____

_____

_____

_____

_____

Gear: _____ x _____

Jetting: _____ / _____

Ignition: _____

Curve: _____

Plug Reading: _____

Session: _____

Hot: Cold: Front Track   Cold: Hot:

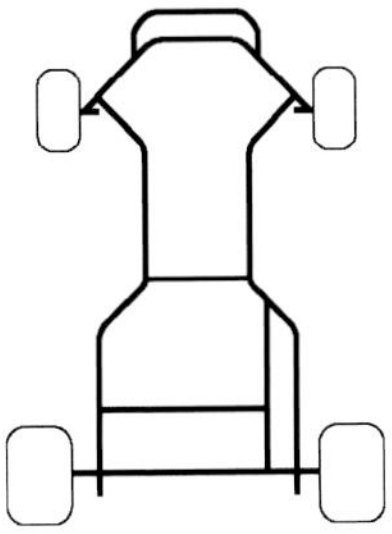

_____   _____   _____   _____

_____   _____   _____   _____

Rear Track

Notes: _____

_____

_____

_____

_____

Gear: _____ x _____

Jetting: _____ / _____

Ignition: _____

Curve: _____

Plug Reading: _____

Session: _____

Hot: Cold: Front Track   Cold: Hot:

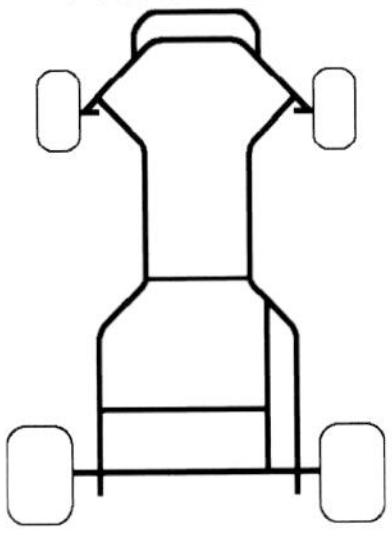

_____   _____   _____   _____

_____   _____   _____   _____

Rear Track

Notes: _____

_____

_____

_____

_____

Gear: _____ x _____

Jetting: _____ / _____

Ignition: _____

Curve: _____

Plug Reading: _____

General Torque Specifications

This chart specifies torque for standard fasteners with standard I.S.O. pitch threads. To avoid warpage, tighten multi-fastener assemblies in a crisscross fashion, in progressive stages, until full torque is reached. Unless otherwise specified, torque specifications call for clean, dry threads. Components should be at room temperature.

A (Nut)	B (Bolt)	TORQUE SPECIFICATION		
		Nm	m•kg	ft•lb
10mm	6mm	6	0.6	4.3
12mm	8mm	15	1.5	11
14mm	10mm	30	3.0	22
17mm	12mm	55	5.5	40
19mm	14mm	85	8.5	61
22mm	16mm	130	13	94

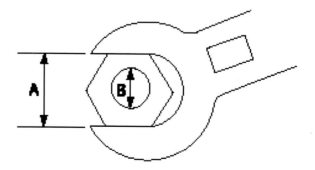

Metric Nut and Bolt Guide

	Hex Head	Flat Head	Socket Cap	Nut / Washer
M6 **Partial Threading:** Fo bolts 25mm to 125mm is 18mm **Drill size: M6 / 15/64** **Thread size: 1.0**	length 18mm	length	length	10 12 6.4
Wrench Size:	M10	T4	T5	M10
M8 **Partial Threading:** For bolts 35mm to 125mm is 22mm **Drill size: M8 / 5/16** **Thread size: 1.25**	length 22mm	length	length	16 16 8.4
Wrench Size:	M13	T5	T6	M13
M10 **Partial Threading:** For bolts 40mm to 125mm is 26mm **Drill size: M10 / 13/32** **Thread size: 1.5**	length 26mm	length	length	20 20 10.5
Wrench Size:	M16	T6	T8	M16

Reprinted courtesy of wewantmetric.com.

Not actual size. For reference purposes only. Consult your dealer for hardware specifications.

Reproduced with permission from Secrets of Speed Publications, Inc. copyright 2005

Secrets of Speed

Check out the other great titles from Memo Gidley and Secrets of Speed Publications

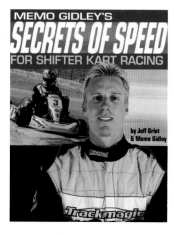

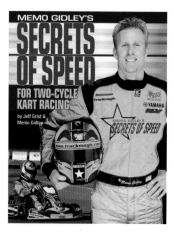

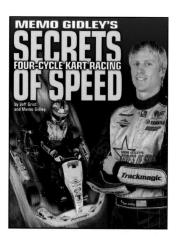

SECRETS OF SPEED FOR SHIFTER KART RACING
February 2003
Soft Cover, 128 pages
ISBN 0-9732595-0-7
$24.95 US

SECRETS OF SPEED FOR TWO-CYCLE KART RACING
February 2004
Soft Cover, 128 pages
ISBN 0-9732595-1-5
$24.95 US

SECRETS OF SPEED FOR FOUR-CYCLE KART RACING
February 2005
Soft Cover, 128 pages
ISBN 0-9732595-2-3
$24.95 US

SECRETS OF SPEED FOR SPEEDWAY KART RACING
October 2006

SECRETS OF SPEED FOR JUNIOR KART RACING
February 2007

Secrets of Speed Publications Inc.
8 Kennedy Road, Grimsby Ontario Canada
L3M 1E7
p. 905.328.7458   f. 905.945.1018
jeff@mgsecretsofspeed.com
Check out www.mgsecretsofspeed.com
for more details on these and other
exciting titles.

dex

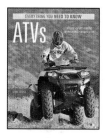

ATVs:
Everything You Need To Know
ISBN 0-7603-2042-X

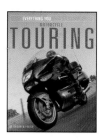

Motorcycle Touring:
Everything You Need To Know
ISBN 0-7603-2035-7

Scooters: Everything You
Need To Know
ISBN 0-7603-2217-1

Speed Secrets:
Professional Race
Driving Techniques
ISBN 0-7603-0518-8

Speed Secrets 2:
More Professional Race
Driving Techniques
ISBN 0-7603-1510-8

Speed Secrets 5:
The Complete Driver
ISBN 0-7603-2289-9

Inner Speed Secrets:
Race Driving Skills, Techniques
& Strategies
ISBN 0-7603-0834-9

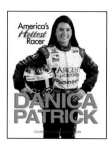

Danica Patrick:
America's Hottest Racer
ISBN 0-7603-2517-0

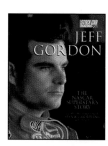

Jeff Gordon
ISBN 0-7603-2178-7